The DOG LOG

The DOG LOG

AN ACCIDENTAL MEMOIR *of*
YAPPING YORKIES,
QUARRELING NEIGHBORS,
and the
UNLIKELY FRIENDSHIPS
THAT SAVED MY LIFE

RICHARD LUCAS

CHICAGO
REVIEW
PRESS

Copyright © 2019 by Richard Lucas
All rights reserved
Published by Chicago Review Press Incorporated
814 North Franklin Street
Chicago, Illinois 60610
ISBN 978-1-64160-118-4

Library of Congress Cataloging-in-Publication Data
Names: Lucas, Richard, 1965– author.
Title: The dog log : an accidental memoir of yapping yorkies, quarreling
    neighbors, and the unlikely friendships that saved my life / Richard
    Lucas.
Description: Chicago : Chicago Review Press, [2019] | Summary:
    "THE DOG LOG, written as a daily notation to the sheriff's
    department, begins as a simple complaint about a barking dog but
    soon becomes a powerful self-exploration and confessional. It's
    the touching, hilarious and cleverly sneaky memoir of a man in
    Los Angeles who inadvertently rediscovers himself when his elderly
    neighbor falls and he must reluctantly tend to her two badly behaved
    Yorkshire terriers"— Provided by publisher.
Identifiers: LCCN 2019023305 (print) | LCCN 2019023306 (ebook) | ISBN
    9781641601184 (trade paperback) | ISBN 9781641601191 (adobe pdf) |
    ISBN 9781641601214 (epub) | ISBN 9781641601207 (kindle edition)
Subjects: LCSH: Yorkshire terrier—Anecdotes.
Classification: LCC SF429.Y6 L83 2019 (print) | LCC SF429.Y6 (ebook) |
    DDC 636.76—dc23
LC record available at https://lccn.loc.gov/2019023305
LC ebook record available at https://lccn.loc.gov/2019023306

All photos provided by the author
Cover design: Preston Pisellini
Typesetter: Nord Compo

Printed in the United States of America
5 4 3 2 1

To my mom, Elsie, a music teacher, who made sure that the arts were always a part of my life

Author's Note

The Dog Log is a comedic memoir based on the real barking dog log that I began keeping as a record of a relentless yapping Yorkie named Sophie who lived next door. I was even reading from my log at storytelling shows back then to share my plight and foist my frustrations upon innocent audiences around Los Angeles. To construct the overall experiences of that time into a shareable literary narrative, some of the characters, instances, and dialogue are composites, recreations, and/or abstractions; some names, physical descriptions, and occupations have also been changed. Also—for your reading pleasure—the original first eighty-five pages or so of "Sophie is barking . . . Sophie is still barking . . . Sophie is barking again . . . Believe me, Sophie is barking . . ." have been trimmed down to one. *Arf! Arf!*

The DOG LOG

ATTN: West Hollywood Sheriff's Dept.

I live next to a barking dog. It is destroying my life. I've done everything possible, including speaking with the neighbor many times—to no avail. When I initially contacted your department, I was told that I would have to keep a barking dog log to document the problem before you would be able to do anything. And so—as my appeal for your assistance—this will be one of those barking dog logs.

1

October

October 1, 10:15 AM
Dear Sheriff,
Sophie is barking.

10:30 AM
Dear Sheriff,
Sophie is barking.

10:45 AM
Dear Sheriff,
Sophie is barking.

11:00 AM
Barking.

11:15 AM
Barking.

11:30 AM
Barking.

11:45 AM
Barking. Barking. Barking. Day one? Not for me. Sophie's stretched me over the rack for months with her yelps, seized up in some permanent panic like a dog version of Edvard Munch's painting *The Scream* with unseeable sound. And this dog log—noting every bark?—has to be my "scream," my hands against my cheeks, my eyes wide in the terror of the shrieks and sounds, the swirling hurricane of noise pain all around me never ending.

October 13, 3:15 PM
Dear Sheriff,

OK, I let two weeks go by. I couldn't take the impotent fury of writing this log. Just know that Sophie's been making my life worse, daily, with each scalding syllable. But I realize that nothing's going to change unless I do this damn thing. So the system's got me. This'll be my evidence of it all, my word as a citizen, tantamount to sworn testimony henceforth.

I've tried everything, in case you're wondering. Why else would I be doing this? I've tried to talk with the owner—left notes, phone messages—all the neighbor stuff. So please check those off your list.

To make it official, I've left several phone messages already today:

BEEEEEP: "Hello, Irene, it's Richard, next door. Sophie's barking. Fifteen minutes now. If it's the usual, she'll go until you get back. Thanks."
BEEEEEP: "Hi, Irene. Richard. Eleven o'clock. Sophie hasn't stopped. Thanks."
BEEEEEP: "Two o'clock—Sophie's still going. Needs an exorcism. Thanks."

Irene has never acknowledged receiving any of my messages. When we cross paths, she saunters past me as if I were a tree trunk unless I speak to her first, and then she just shouts at me, which is OK for an old lady to do but not for me. That's an inexorable function of reasonable society.

October 14, 11:00 AM
Dear Sheriff,

Drop a hammer on your toes. Now do that forty thousand times, light your hair on fire, have your mother criticize you for all your faults, and punch yourself in the ears until your knuckles bleed. That is living next to Sophie. *Arf. Arf.* All day. Perhaps you might get yourself a recording of a dog barking and enjoy it along with me, won't you? No—you won't.

October 15, 10:00 AM
OK—Sophie's making me nuts. This is ridiculous, two weeks of writing this down. I'm going to call the sheriff's station again today and get this settled.

10:10 AM
That didn't help. The deputy on the phone told me the same frustrating thing that you guys told me in September: "Keep keeping a log." He said sometimes a dog might be sick, have allergies or some new stress, whatever, so you don't want to jump right into the fray. And sometimes people lie to screw with neighbors they don't like, *blah, blah, blah.* So I could end up needing maybe up to six months of dog log if an intervention is needed, or it goes to court, or something like that, so that I can show "that the problem indeed exists and persists." He offered to send a letter, a warning of a fine, but said many ignore them, so it takes a lot of time. *Yeah, half the time Irene has a week's worth of mail jammed up in her mail slot.* In the meantime, he said, "It might not last all that long. Sometimes life can change. You'd be surprised."

I could tell you don't want to get in the middle of it, and that he wanted to get me off the phone.

11:00 AM

Exist and persist. I'll never forget those words, especially since they mean *I'll never see you again because you won't persist with this, and so you don't exist to me.*

Would you tell the owner of a liquor store to keep a log if a guy kept running in to his place waving a gun day after day? Your cars shouldn't have A Tradition of Service on them—they should say, See You in Six Months. You want the person to crack and move away, don't you? Do you know what rents are like out there? I do exist. And I will persist. Justice is supposed to be swift. As Clarence Darrow said, "Mercy is the highest attribute of man." Where is the mercy? I can't concentrate anymore. I'm sleeping about as well as a clock, and my emotions are in a popcorn popper. I've been gaining weight, stress-eating Cheetos. I have a bad knee, so I haven't been able to run for over a year, and this isn't helping. My face is breaking out. Darkened eyes, sinking jowls. Have you ever cried at nothing, Sheriff?

And I'm not going to have you guys start with the notes. It won't do any good, because the dog won't change, and Irene won't do anything because she hasn't yet, and she won't pay a fine. I'm sure she wouldn't be able to. And then what? And do I want the dog wrenched from her grasp at the front door to go to a shelter or something? No. I just want things fixed. And what a worse nightmare Irene herself would become on top of the problem with the barking. She'd probably call the cops on me for some made-up thing in retribution, like my TV was too loud or something. And then what?

But if it continues, I worry that when I eventually turn in this log, you'll just glance at the first page to see the date, then turn to the last page to see that date, and then coldly note on some Civil Disturbance Report Form that "Resident claimed dog issue for six-month period," and that'd be it. But there's so much more to it than that.

Look, though—OK, I'm not crazy. I'm fine. Life is fine. What do you think, complaining about Sophie gives meaning to my life? Let me tell you—I'm a revolutionary. I am standing in front of the tank with this dog log. I'll document what so many fellow citizens suffer through in silence—languishing out there—forcing themselves to incorporate noises into their daily lives like the burning crawl of a skin disease. I say this: I am Richard Lucas, and I am going to make dogs quiet and neighbors be neighborly!

Maybe I need to do something bigger, quicker. Self-immolate. Go out onto the front grass, douse myself, and offer the world an altruistic act of martyrdom, spread the light of the dharma like the great Bodhisattva Medicine King so that you and the authorities of the world can focus on this repression that I, and all other decent citizens whose peaceful lives are ruined by barking dogs, can no longer endure. Let my burning flesh rise up to the sky in a glorious gray column of rebellion. (I don't care that the city council's trying to outlaw outdoor barbecues.) Come, good friends, cook your hamburgers, your hot dogs, your Tofurky chorizos here above the flames of my burning carcass! Bring marshmallows and songs of celebration to the spectacle of my timely death, and join in my cause!

October 16, 4:00 PM
Dear Sheriff,

Barking all afternoon. Sophie's a Yorkshire terrier. Yorkshire must have been one of the original portals to hell. She barks like she has three heads. It's like the screeching metal emergency-braking wheels of a freight train that's about to hit a school bus filled with screaming kids.

Six months—so now until April if need be—like being handed a six-month form to fill out. Bureaucrats are assholes. OK, you're not assholes, sorry. Well, you're not a bureaucrat. And you're also not an asshole, I'm sure (though I might suggest that many in your department could work on their first-impressions skills). I'm a good person here. But it feels like war. Me against Sophie. Maybe it's me against you. I hope not. I'm fighting for peace here—not necessarily peace of mind, because you can't provide that—but peace around my mind, which is my right.

October 17, 3:15 PM

I can't believe how freakin' hot it is today. It's supposed to be autumn, isn't it? Barking is so random. Some noises, like with my neighbors—Casino's stereo or Jazmine's feather-sensitive car alarm— you can blend into your mental background because they're consistent sounds, and you know it'll eventually stop. But my head can't create a formula on Sophie. Plus, today her voice is swollen with the vengeful power of the North Sea crashing against the Cliffs of Moher.

October 18, 2:00 PM

Since you're the sheriff, I'll draw you a police sketch: Sophie is black and brown like a blood-soaked turd, mostly black along her head and caped over her back like she's wearing a Darth Vader hand-puppet costume. Beady little glassy brown eyes snarl from her pointy face, and her sweaty black nose twitches constantly like a divining rod to the devil's lake of fire. She's tiny, smaller than a computer mouse. Irene, her owner, a bonkers old woman in her mid-to-horrible seventies, once told me that Sophie weighs three pounds. She would stand about ten inches on her hind legs, like a rat. I've never seen her walk, because Irene snuggles her against her bosom when they're outside.

"She's just healing. She fell off of the front step," Irene says.

There are two tiny front steps out there, Sheriff; she couldn't handle a tiny step to the ground—and so she can't walk, I guess.

As far as I can tell from the huge area of staining, Sophie wets herself freely on Irene's black T-shirt dress as they shuffle along, and Irene cradles tissues under Sophie's behind to almost-catch her random defecations. Sometimes, when she doesn't want to disturb Sophie's sleep, Irene carries her, preening, in a little wicker handbasket.

"It's her *le petit boudoir*," she says.

It's a wicker basket for a picnic of grime and filth, because Sophie must never get a bath. She's an animal so pathetic that if St. Francis of Assisi were to see her coming along, even he would find an excuse to cross the street to avoid her. The only sign of color one can see is the bite-sized red ribbon that is clipped on her head like Satan's horns to pin back her overgrown hair. But even it is damp and dull with months of unwashed dog-hair grease that has soaked its shiny crimson down to darkened, drooping joylessness.

They say that dogs often resemble their owners, so now you have an idea of Irene as well, except that her long, unwashed hair is darkened yellow / dull white and wrapped and coiffed in a deflated bun that sits atop her head like a rotting grapefruit. And, of course, Sophie's injury might have something to do with the barking now, but she barked before that, too. She's just a plain old maniacally squealing infliction, and she'll only be louder when she gets her legs back.

October 19, 11:00 AM

You probably think I'm an asshole now because I made fun of Sophie's stupid broken legs yesterday. I don't even know if they're broken. I wish I could break her legs sometimes. No I don't. Sorry. I'm sure they're not. Irene wouldn't just let the dog be enfeebled, right? Maybe it's some neurological problem that causes her barking? I like animals. They're fine. But this disturbance is a legal problem, and Irene won't take responsibility.

Please don't think I'm an asshole. I'm just so frustrated. And me being an asshole shouldn't have anything to do with the law. I said I'm freakin' sorry. I'm sure this is a wealth and privilege issue, typical Los Angeles—where those born with golden Pampers on their butts get all the opportunity and the breaks. I guarantee no famous person has ever had to turn in a six-month barking dog log, or any sordid calendar of torture. And here I am, a common, humble man, scratching the days off my cell wall with a chiseled-down pebble like Dr. Alexandre Manette. Sorry, Sheriff, I used to be an English teacher—Dr. Manette was the old man held prisoner in the Tower of London at the beginning of Charles Dickens's novel *A Tale of Two Cities*. You know—"It was the best of times, it was the worst of times." If you haven't read it (maybe you have) you should, you'd love it. I'm living in the *beast* of times. Seconds pass like a slug on sandpaper. Ugh, it's late. I'm drinking wine, and I'm mixing metaphors now like T. S. Eliot. Are you much of a grammar wonk, Sheriff? Syntax? Does anyone care about rules anymore?

October 20, 10:00 PM

My girlfriend, Roxy, and I just had a fight because of Sophie. I'd asked her to talk to Irene about the barking, because I thought a woman-to-woman conversation might get somewhere. Roxy said, "No, I don't particularly feel like getting yelled at." Remember—she yells.

"That's the point. I don't think she'll yell at a woman. She sort of likes you."

"But I don't like her," she said.

"Yes, you do. You guys chat."

"Yes, I have spasms of pity for her and seconds of passing chit-chat," she said, "but I don't feel like getting into any kind of a confrontation today."

"You and I are in kind of a confrontation right now," I fumbled.

"Because you're being a baby," she said. "Look, this is something you're going to have to deal with on your own. Call Randall, finally."

Randall's our landlord, Sheriff.

"He'd just try to have the dog taken away because they hate each other."

A little history: When Irene moved in she cut a doggy door into the bedroom wall. He made her close it up. They've been mortal enemies ever since. "Does it make me less of a man that I don't want a dog taken away from an old woman?" I asked.

"No, but all your complaining and the emotional high-wire act do," she said. "You know what, maybe if this were *our* place, I'd talk with her."

Roxy's too good a chess player for me. She could turn a discussion about the spices in the spaghetti sauce into a *Why aren't we living together yet?* squabble. It's complicated.

October 21, 11:00 AM

I saw Irene out back near her car this morning when I was taking out the trash. I mentioned Sophie.

"Well, I don't know what I'm supposed to do about it!" she barked. "The only option is to get rid of my dog, and I'm not going to do that!"

"I wasn't saying to get rid of her. You're not taking me seriously."

"When Sophie barks, she thinks she's protecting me. I'm all alone."

Useless. No one's listening to me. I dumped my trash and came back in.

October 22, 3:00 PM

You wouldn't believe the suggestions I get. My older sister, Ally, sent me a link this morning to an electronic collar that shocks a dog in a "nonharmful way" when it barks, reverse-Pavlovian style. Ninety-five dollars. I printed it out and showed it to Irene by her front door. (She didn't invite me inside, not that I'd ever want her to.)

"Get away from me with that medieval torture device," she said. "I will not hang that dreadful millstone around my Sophie's neck. Those things should be illegal."

Of course, nothing about what I'm going through is dreadful or illegal, right? Sophie's a twisted masochist who'd only groove on the buzzes anyhow. It does happen, you know. People feed off physical pain as a way to avoid emotional issues, such as our universal loneliness. People even "cut" themselves. I bet it can happen with dogs. Surely Sophie causes herself pain barking hour after hour. I think if it were seasoned with a little shock, it'd only lead to more emotional masturbation. Anyway, all the suggestions involve buying something, and I'm drawing the line: a person should not have to spend money for a problem that's caused by—and should be solved by—a neighbor. This is a human problem, and Irene needs to solve it. There needs to be better enforcement of kindness and consideration among neighbors. I am going to defeat the curse of proximity.

October 23, 12:00 PM

Irene's door just slammed shut. The guillotine. Sophie started up with her groping, baleful tragedy: *Please don't go!* or whatever she's bitching about in her canine ignorance. You know what, Sophie? Irene left you again. But it's not forever. Why can't you get that through your pumpkin-seed brain? What locks you in? If only I could find the key, then I'd be a hero.

October 24, 11:00 AM

I'll tell you what, I'll try again. I'll go knock on Irene's door and try to talk to her. I guarantee she'll just fight with me. Be right back.

12:25 PM

Not home. My knocking made Sophie go nuts, so now I'm paying the price for trying. And my arm is killing me. It feels like I'm being branded in a cattle chute. OK, I'll leave her a note—another of my many. For the record: "Dear Irene, just wanted to let you know that Sophie barked a great deal today. I'm not feeling well. Is there any way that you can train her to be quiet? Thank you, Richard." We'll see if she responds. She won't.

5:50 PM

She got home about an hour ago—no response. Told you. Burns me up. What is a person thinking when they get a note and ignore it? You can't *not* read it? Only the darkest of souls.

1:00 AM

Not sleeping much anymore. Exhausted. There's a single wall that connects our apartments. It's so thin that it doesn't separate our worlds, it actually blends them. Some days, I feel like a portal opens up and a psychic bridge spans from Sophie to me, spurring me to want to bark as well. I'm becoming a basket case, maybe a wicker basket case just as she is—Sophie, my mysterious and shocking partner in pain. It's sympathetic vibration. Have you heard of that,

Sheriff? If there are, say, two guitars in a room and a note's plucked on one, that same note will ring out on the other. That's us. What was hers is now also mine—ours. I wonder if sometimes I'm not more with Sophie than against her?

October 26, 9:30 PM

I fantasize about killing Sophie. Big surprise? You carry a gun, Sheriff, don't tell me you don't think about your own power over life. I could do it so quickly too, even painlessly—get her neck between my thumb and index finger, strangle her as easily as crushing graham crackers. You know what? I'd love to bark her to death, a half hour screaming at her. What a passionate opera we'd produce together.

The irony is, I have experience in conflict resolution. I taught for seven years in South L.A. at a high school where they had to employ two armed school police. I was hit in the head with brass knuckles breaking up a fight and I didn't miss a day. In teacher training, we spent more time hypothesizing solutions to "conflict scenarios" than we did lesson planning *Huck Finn* or unconvoluting English grammar. You think I don't have patience? I have years of dealing with untenable scenarios. I'm not going to kill Sophie, for God's sake. I wonder, though, if I carried a gun . . .

11:00 PM

Late. Officially out of bourbon. It helps with the anxiety worms that crawl under my skin, vein to artery to corpuscle. There's a terrible stinging down my left arm. And like a werewolf, I hear every drip of sound in the crying silence as loud as the smack of a hammer pounding nails into a cross.

Ally called tonight to tell me about my niece's violin recital. All I could talk about was Sophie. Then we hung up. I had to call her back to ask again why she'd called. See what this does to me?

"You're too stressed. I can tell you've been drinking," she said. "I'm going to send you some jujube seed and plum flower." Ally's an herbalist / massage therapist / Eastern Healer / everything's-sunshine type up near Portland.

"Does Sophie have karma?" I asked.

"Geez. You're obsessed."

"Does she?"

Ally tells me, "First of all, karma says that a person experiences 'that to which they pay the most attention.' No one pays more attention to negative stimuli than you, freak."

"Before you think that I can just walk away from Sophie, understand that her barking is paying attention to me. It penetrates my attention span."

"Because you choose to focus on it—"

"It dwells in my dwelling, like a spouse—it can't be ignored."

"Unless it's Mom and Dad."

"There's some karma for ya."

"Yep."

"Well, karmically, Sophie may be the reincarnation of someone who'd done despicable things—"

"So, like, Jack the Ripper may now be Sophie the Barker."

"Could be."

"I want to know—will Sophie someday pay for what she's doing to me?"

"That's awful. Karmic revenge? On an animal? You have to turn off your negative energy," she said.

"I'm being fed negative energy every day. You talk as though reincarnation is a reliable system of karmic justice. So, is it or not?"

"Sophie's an innocent animal. She has no awareness of her soul."

"But she has freedom of the will and, with that, a responsibility to herself and others regarding her choices. She can choose to bark or not."

"Dogs don't choose," she said.

"They certainly do. They can love someone, bite someone, kill them, or kiss them. Freedom of the will, Ally."

"Well, St. Augustine, now you're asking what's been preordained and how much choice any of us really has versus fate."

"Yes. Fate—destiny—like in Oedipus Rex—I'm going to gouge out my own eyes because of this tragic fate befallen unto me. Actually, my ears would be better to get rid of—a double Van Gogh."

"Sophie is not choosing things, as you drunkenly theorize. She's a result. You have the opportunity to stop further result in your own life by having a positive attitude and sending positivity out into the universe."

At that point, I ended the conversation, because I can't stand being told to be positive. You try it.

October 31, 12:25 PM

Happy Bark-o-ween. There are actually two dogs over at Irene's— how spooky is that? Along with Sophie, Irene has a second Yorkie named Nelson to uncare for. He can walk. He's a mute, the best kind of Yorkie. He doubles the amount of feces-stuck scruff that Irene has to not wash. I don't know if his vocal cords have been snipped (which, as much as I hate barking, would be horrible) or if he just chooses not to talk, but his monastic silence is a welcome gift at this point. I wish he could persuade Sophie to take the vows.

We're on North Hayworth, between Willoughby and Romaine. Irene and I each rent small, one-bedroom cottages attached by our wall. I think they were originally built for veterans returning from WWII. A hero may have once lived here. We have two neighbors in the back: Casino, a tall, handsome, affable, truth-bending, all-too-charming ladies' man and DJ—I call him the Black Don Juan (if Don Juan could also spin records and make ladies' panties drop, including your grandma if she has her dancing shoes on)—and Jazmine, a heavyset Asian girl in her midtwenties with an affinity for tight pink clothing, sparkles on everything, and leaving her Camaro parked in the driveway so that no one can get in or out without asking her. They live in the same type of units as we do. No one above, below, or on three sides, a step away from architectural paradise.

Ten years ago I jumped on this place, even though Randall, the landlord, was clearly a tight bird. He has deep-set eyes that prowl above an anachronistically thick black-and-white mustache that resembles the brow of a skunk, and he never stops studying you with a derisive suspicion, as if you're secretly concocting ways to make him spend money. When his poking voice cawed, "You're credit report is OK. The apartment is yours," I was ecstatic. This place is small, though. That's an element of why Roxy and I don't live together.

I'm a lucky man, Sheriff. Roxy's the complete combination of all the great aspects of every woman I've ever been attracted to. Really—smart, funny, ambitious, caring, athletic, beautiful—let me put funny in there twice, because, damn, she makes me laugh. I mean it—all the way back to my first crush, Miss Jenkins, my second-grade teacher—Roxy is all of them. When I met her, I had that relaxing sensation of knowing that the search of the heart had ended. We've looked at some two-bedroom apartments in the past couple months, but there's nowhere we can afford right now to live the way we picture. It's causing a little friction, I suppose. We've been together for seven years. We'll get past this. Roxy has a good job as a high school guidance counselor. We used to work at the same school. That's where we met when I was teaching. I was a musician, too, writing songs and playing out at night. That's why I came to L.A. after college in Pittsburgh, originally. I eventually chose to leave teaching to put more time into my music, and I became self-employed. I do graphic design, self-taught: websites, logos, brochures, etc. I could always draw, so it made sense. Business, however, can be unsteady. That makes Roxy uneasy and rental applications tricky. I just need a break, you know? Something good to fall my way. Besides, if I were to move, who's to say that the new situation would be any better neighbor-wise?

November

November 1, 12:25 PM

Dia de los Muertos. My Dia de los Barking. I don't know why Randall
didn't manage to evict Irene when she did the doggy door thing.
If only . . . Maybe he receives some tax benefit from giving housing
to someone on disability? Oh—Irene claims she had a brain tumor
once. She does seem to be forever on the verge of tipping over like
a toddler wearing her mother's heels. I have no doubt that, if push
came to shove, Randall would either have the dogs taken away or
he'd force her to move. I don't want to be the person who's respon-
sible for something so devastating.

I'm a good person, Sheriff. In my father's last years after his
stroke, our cat, Buttons, grew old with him, lounging on his lap,
giving him someone to talk to and an exchange of affection that he
couldn't get from any other source. (He wasn't the sweetest guy.)
Certainly I don't want you guys to storm into Irene's with a SWAT
team and break that up. I just wish you could pressure her a bit in

17

your unique way, back me up, make her get someone to train the dog or something.

November 2, 11:00 AM

I can't take it. I'm walking to the Coffee Commissary on Fairfax to work. What am I paying rent for, by the way, if I'm pushed out just to get caffeine in my blood and earn a living? I have a right to stay within my own walls.

11:30 AM

Everything in this place smells like pumpkin and cinnamon swirling in warm bagel pretentiousness like a corporatist happiness cloud to dull the masses. Took forever to get coffee because of the line. How are all these people not at jobs right now? Four dollars a cup? Holy mackerel—every day that'd add up to eighty dollars a month. This is nuts. It's cold here, and elbow-to-elbow. All the chatter, too. I can't work this way. Worse, I just got a phone call from a client. When I answered, I guess because of the noise, she said, "Is everything OK, Richard?"

"Oh, sorry," I said. "No, everything's fine."

And then she gave me the "Are you sure?" question. There's no recovery from the "Are you sure?" in the business world. "We kind of have an emergency today, but it sounds like you're busy, so I'll get someone else."

"No, no, no, I'm just at a café, and I—" And she hung up. So, I'm losing money today because I'm not home, and everything's an emergency.

12:30 PM

I don't know how long they let you sit here. I'm trying to work on a poster for a play, a sadly wasted staging of Sam Shepard's great *True West*. It's a story of sibling rivalry, envy, and power, Sheriff. It's being produced by two actors, basically like a "showcase" to get agents, the ruin of small theater in this town. These dudes have enough money to rent a theater, hire a publicist, etc., but, of course, "almost no money" for me to create the art, and it's an emergency. I take every job because I'm bailing my lifeboat, fighting a quixotic battle against debt, taxes, everything. Had a bad run lately. Nothing adds up quicker than minus signs. I'm sort of trying to hide that from Roxy. This sucks. I don't have any resource books with me, nothing. I'm just sitting here wired on some kind of methampheta-caffeine writing this log, surrounded by unisex-yoga-pantsed narcissists. How can these people preen and whine at the same time? I'm going home.

2:00 PM
Holy fuck—someone broke into my place while I was gone. *See what I get for leaving?* Popped the front window open in broad daylight. And this is a decent neighborhood. Looks like all they got was one of my guitars, which sucks, but it was just a practice jammer collecting dust because I don't play much anymore. Didn't seem to have gotten back into the bedroom where the others are stored. Fuck! If they'd gotten my computer I'd be totally fucked. Why isn't Sophie protecting me, huh?

7:00 PM
I called 9-1-1. You guys came and dusted for fingerprints, etc. I wonder if one of them was you? Sophie was barking up a lung.

"That's quite a little bear you've got next door. Ha," your deputy laughed. "She must be stressed with all this commotion, poor thing."

"Actually, she's being normal. I'm stressed."

"Ha. Can you check on her? Sounds like she's all alone, poor thing."

Again with the *poor thing*. "She's actually a pretty rotten dog."

"Well, it's been a rough day around here for everyone, I suppose." Then he left me to the barking. Oh, he recommended I put bars on the windows. Randall will never go for that.

8:00 PM
I talked to Roxy and told her about this totally shitty day. I wanted to go to her place, because I didn't feel like being alone. But she said her

roommate was having a party or something. "Karen's got friends over
in the living room. I really want to try to get some sleep tonight anyhow. My stomach doesn't feel great." So I'm home still. Long night.

November 3, 7:00 PM

I called Randall today about the bars. "Well, I'm afraid that, if indeed
we were to put bars on your windows, which do face the street, it
would affect property values for the entire neighborhood," he trilled.
What a bastard. I should sue him. "If indeed . . ." He always says that
when a money issue comes up. Is it at all ironic to you, Sheriff, that I
can't get bars put onto the windows of my own prison? Were you here?

I've got to ask—who are you? Are you married? Kids? Whose
job is it to read citizen-generated journals about domestic distur-
bances? Someone's going to read it, right? Is there a legal library or
somewhere you can at least get comfortable lighting? Maybe it's a
rookie thing. I've heard that all new deputies have to start out with
two years at the county jail. I've never understood that—putting
the least experienced officers right in with criminals—like the guy
who has my guitar. Well, everyone in jail isn't a criminal; it's mostly
pretrial, right? But you assume their guilt. Be honest—these men in
county jumpsuits, walking silently, single file, hands in pockets from
cell block to cell block. I know. I've been to the jail. Wouldn't that
affect you in the worst way?

Have you been a guard at the jail? Is it possible you're in a guard
booth there right now? Look out at those inmates. I'm one of them
when Sophie starts barking—yet I've committed no crime. Yet.

You studied criminal psychology, right? You know, I could mor-
ally justify a Raskolnikovian higher purpose in ridding myself of
our problem. Raskolnikov is the main character in Russian novelist
Fyodor Dostoyevsky's novel *Crime and Punishment.* Raskolnikov acts
on his theory of different moralities for "ordinary" versus "extraordi-
nary" people, regarding the murder of his landlord. You should read
it. It deepens one's understanding of the effect on your morals when
presented with a major dilemma like I've been. Reading some of this
literature could make you a more thoughtful public servant. In fact,

you might set up a little reading club in the department to discuss it. I could give you a whole list of books. For example, take Jean-Paul Sartre, who wrote about the "moral imperative." When up against an obstacle, he suggests that a person pause and "assume that all mankind will use you as a model and will make the identical choice in the same situation"—that is, pretend everyone in the world were to do what you are thinking of doing. What would the world be like then?

Well, I've had many people tell me to do horrible things. My friend Tom: "We grew up next to a beagle that wouldn't shut up. One day Dad put ground-up glass in his food on their back porch, and the problem was solved in twenty-four hours." Those are morals ravaged by exacerbation. I bet Sophie's a finicky eater. Anyway—no matter.

Did you know that there's no word for "the murder of an animal," like *homicide, patricide, suicide*? I just looked it up online. How could it not get a word? Of course, now the Internet has a record of me searching "murder a dog." I should type in something about "liking dogs" to balance out my browser history.

November 4, 10:00 AM

Irene is the neighbor in question, Sophie's owner. (I know the West Hollywood City Council voted 3–0 to ban the term *pet owner* in favor of *pet guardian*, but that's so ridiculous it makes my eyeballs boil.) I mentioned she lives on disability. Don't cry for her already, Sheriff. Believe me, she's selfish, arrogant, and ill-tempered. Yes, people with disabilities can be jerks, too—welcome to the human race. Plus, as you know, Irene yells at me when I mention Sophie. I suffer from neighbor abuse! Anyhow, I'm losing work productivity because of this—so I'm virtually disabled too. What are you going to do about that?

I thought things might have turned out better around here. Early on the second morning after I'd moved in, a knock at the door invaded my privacy. I threw on a T-shirt and opened the door to see a small, round, aged woman in a long dirty black cotton housedress, which looked as if she'd been wearing it for several weeks of chain gang work. The morning sun rim-lit her ostrich-egg figure, silhouetting her face through my still-closed screen door.

"Good morning," she said, "I hope I'm not disturbing you." That's what people always say when they're disturbing you. Her voice sounded torn in half, and her overprojection of it hit my ears like feedback at a Van Halen concert. "I just wanted to let you know that I'm the very best neighbor you're ever going to have," she offered.

I smiled and thought, *This could be good news.* "Why do you say that?" I asked, still not knowing her name.

"Because I'm blind in one eye and deaf in one ear."

I'm not half bad at guessing riddles, Sheriff, but I would have never gotten that one. And how do you respond to that? "Wow, that's fantastic—too bad you're not full-on Helen Keller, you could be famous!"? But "Oh? That's just awful," was all I sputtered out. It wasn't important, however, because her determination to tell me her story was not to be daunted.

In some circumstances, this might have been an appropriate moment for me to invite her in for a cup of tea, but tea gives me a sour stomach, and, more important, I had no interest in establishing a spontaneous tea date relationship with the ancient, intruding busybody next door. Once you give them a little Orange Zinger, Sheriff, they keep coming back.

So, remaining outside, she jabbered on, explaining that her blindness, deafness, and vertigo, which had all colluded to quicksand her into a most unjust poverty, stemmed from a brain tumor. "I had it removed, of course."

"Often that's the best course of action," I concurred.

"I'm OK, but it left me unable to work anymore or function much. I used to be very successful," she asserted from behind her exaggerated Jackie O sunglasses, which, thankfully, hid the mystery of her one-sided blindness, what Edgar Allan Poe might have imagined as the "vulture eye," as she prattled on. Maybe it was the slight slur dragging her speech along—likely a result of the tumor—but something about this worn package of human being presenting itself had prejudiced me against any belief that she'd ever been "very successful." Was that unfair of me? *There but for the grace of God go I*, I reminded myself. My mother used to say that. And if I were to be diagnosed today with a tumor such as this woman's, I wouldn't be able to tell anyone that I'd ever been any kind of "great success" before its discovery.

And a great success she claimed to be. "I'm Irene. I used to be a lawyer, Vassar and UCLA. I owned my own family law practice in Beverly Hills. I worked over three thousand divorces. So, if you're getting a divorce, you can call me," she smiled.

I wanted a divorce from this conversation. *I guess not inviting her in for tea isn't stopping this from happening. Her "greatest neighbor ever" status is quickly coming into question*, I thought.

The unconnected, I assumed concocted, and unwelcome details of her life came flying at me now like a snapped rack of pool balls, and all I could do was stand there on the other side of the screen, listening like a priest at a confessional, gathering up the shadowed image of her face through the moiré. Occasionally I tossed in an "Oh" or an "Uh-huh." Perhaps I should have offered up a handful of Hail Marys as well.

"I had eighth-row season tickets to the Showtime Lakers at the Forum, you know, Magic and Kareem," her words now frolicking with pride. "My second husband has a wing named after him at Cedars-Sinai because he donated $12 million to them in 1974. My third husband and I divorced after I found him in bed with a young, blond-haired man who looked just like me. I saw him and yelled, 'Well, he's just me with a penis!'"

My appreciative bewilderment at her one-phrase histories was zapped to clarity by her use of the word *penis*.

"I wanted nothing from that bastard," she went on. "So, I just walked away, took nothing. I'd had success of my own. I was a big women's-libber back then. Look where that got me—Gloria Steinem, good Lord. Well, I could use that money now. Who knew?" With that she let out a laugh/sigh that could have been the Frankenstein monster's last breath under the funeral pyre.

"You seem like a pretty independent lady," I said, trying to be charming, but it came out as pure condescension, exaggerated by the extra volume I was throwing aloft to find her good ear. She ignored it. Maybe she didn't hear me, or maybe she didn't want to be talked down to. I wondered if she was mad at me. Then she stumbled for a moment, just standing there, and steadied herself with her hand against the doorknob.

"Do you need help?"

"No, it's just the vertigo," she said. "I'm fine." She drew a deep breath and continued on, "Oh, I had a beautiful house on Coldwater Canyon and a staff of six at my office."

Lies, lies, lies, I thought. *None of this is even remotely possible, and a continual fiction such as this might have no boundaries whatsoever. I have to get this door closed. I just moved in. Give it some time, Irene. Give me my space.*

"I hope you don't mind my plants and flowers," she said, referring to her attempt at a potted Eden that intrudes on our walkway. But it is pretty, in a dingy way, and what else close to beauty does this woman have? "Randall won't let me grow anything in his precious front yard, so I have to do it all in planters."

She's trying to draw me outside, I thought. *No way, no garden tour. Too much, too fast.* "I hope they don't attract bugs," I warned. Look, I was open to the possibility of a guarded friendship some day with an occasional lemon water and sugar-free cookie, but *Everything in due time* seemed the smarter plan. We were new neighbors, and we needed good fences.

November 5, 12:30 PM

Irene and her garden. This morning she was gardening out front, watering her plants. She had her little blue watering can and her hand spade, but what she'd forgotten, unfortunately, was her pants. Nothing but a ragged black T-shirt and cream-colored Hindenburg panties.

"Good morning, Richard," she said, her pale cheeks reflecting the yellows of her marigolds.

"Good morning to you, Irene. What a beautiful day."

"It's too hot," burst out her auto-complaint.

"Yes, it's hot. It's hot for November—but not too hot for pants."

"Oh, who cares. No one's looking at me."

"I'm looking."

"Well, stop looking. I'm only going to be out here for ten minutes."

"Irene, I insist you put on pants."

"Oh, you're being silly."

"I'm deadly silly, Irene."

She laughed. Sophie'd been barking away.

"Don't you hear Sophie?"

"What's she doing?"

What? "Umm—she's going nuts behind your door."

"Oh, it must not be too loud because I can't hear it," she said.

"You're half deaf, remember?"

"Ha!" she laughed. "Sometimes I forget."

"But you hear me. If you can hear me, then you can hear her."

"Oh, I can't believe such a tiny dog can be such a big problem to you," she said, laughing. "She only weighs three pounds."

"It's all throat."

"Listen," she went on, "if she's barking when I'm not home, it's only because she's lonely. I should give you a key, and then you can go over and visit her. She'd like that."

"I'd pack her up and ship her to a hungry family in North Korea."

"Oh, you're just mean." And the humor vanished. "She's not that loud, get over it."

"Well, please get her to stop. You're a very selfish person, do you know that? And, I reiterate, please put on pants."

Good morning, world.

Sophie visitations? I'm not a dog babysitter. I have no intention of spending time with it over there staring at me—and probably barking. I'd make Lennie Small—the way that he squeezes small animals to death in Steinbeck's *Of Mice and Men*—look like Dr. Dolittle. Her idea is entrapment!

I get so embarrassed when I let myself get angry like this and I can't let it go—makes me feel awful. Maybe it's a problem. I get it from my father. He was a drinker. We had to do our best to avoid him each night when he came home. Saturdays were the worst. He'd rant and rave, alone in the kitchen, about his job, the house, each of us. "The Saturday Evening Soliloquies," we called them. "No communication in the house," he'd say to himself over and over. Who could communicate with that? Mom encouraged us to stay at friends' houses on Saturday nights.

This is complicated to say, but I know he loved us. He just was a hardened, nonloving person. He showed love by paying the mortgage on our small house. He'd bought it in 1966 for $10,000, yet the payments were still a struggle sometimes, five kids and all. I'm not him. I'm just saying. I'm not him.

November 6, 12:30 PM

Casino just told me that Irene scratched my car out back—two days ago, apparently—and no one told me. He saw her leave a huge gash on my driver's-side door while she was parking. He said, "She just got out of her car and walked away." When he stopped her, she begged him not to tell me about it. That's the kind of person we're dealing with, Sheriff.

When I went back there, I flipped. We called Irene outside. She admitted everything but was snarky as can be. "You shouldn't take things so seriously," she said. "I'll pay to have your car fixed."

Lies. What am I going to do, scrape off of her Social Security checks? I'd rather her buy a pair of pants. All I said was, "If you can't manage back here, why don't you just park on the street?"

She turned to walk away.

"Where are you going?"

"You're yelling at me, and I won't be yelled at. I'm leaving!"

"I'm not yelling," I yelled. "I just want to make sure you can hear me."

"I said I'd pay for your precious car," said the portly, petulant, unwashed prom queen, and she blithely waddled away in her protective nest of senior haze. My anger blasted in me like a hot virus. So, I still drive an old Integra—so what? This decrepit old woman is going to give me shit about my car? Her Honda Civic has personalized license plates: 2URKEEZ. Vanity plates for a peripherally impaired, side-swiping menace? She's vain enough to pay for those but not vain enough to give the dogs a bath. California is a disgusting place.

Frustrated, I turned to Casino, who stood there, arms crossed, shaking his head. "What?" I insisted.

"That went bad," he judged in his smooth, younger–Lou-Rawls baritone, glass-of-Glenlivet-on-the-rocks voice.

"Well, how else was it going to go?"

"You've got to check your anger, man. She's an old lady."

"You know she shouldn't be driving."

"Well, yeah," he said, "but there's no way to stop her. Nothing tougher than taking the car keys away from an old person. It's like pulling a tooth out of a tiger's mouth. Plus, you know where she goes every day?"

"To the vampire clinic for blood transfusions?"

"No. You don't know? She goes to hospitals and stuff to visit hospice patients. So if she stops driving, they stop getting those visits."

"Are you serious?"

"Yep," he said. "So, it's tough to get too mad at her the way that you do all the time."

At that point, all my anger, topped with the sixteen-inch laceration on my car and the Nuremberg judgment from Casino, had never seethed with more fluid ferocity. But Casino jammed a cork in it with the hospice announcement. How can I be angry at someone who's volunteering like that? Our little city-within-a-city has an inordinate need for hospice, as you know. It's very sad. And, by the way—what volunteering do I do? None, Sheriff, none. I sit around simmering with sorrow for myself and trying to pay the rent. But it's her leaving her apartment that's the cause of my problems. I'm in a bear trap. Do you see why I don't tell Randall and have her dogs taken away?

When I told Roxy about it, she said, "Oh, what a sweet person."

"Well, I wouldn't want her visiting me in hospice. What about my car?"

"Really, Richard?" was all she said.

November 7, 10:50 AM

One day after confessing to hitting my car, Irene has the chutzpah to ask me for help with hers. "Richard, can you take a look at my car?" beckoned the creaky voice of the cretinous care-faker outside my door. "It won't start."

Great, I thought, *then you won't be able to leave, and Sophie may stay calm, at least when other dogs aren't walking by.* "What's wrong with it?"

"How would I know? Can you take a look?"

"OK," I say. And why not? I can't refuse, now that I know she's probably going to visit patients at hospice. We went out to her car. I turned the key—no sound. Dead battery, like my soul. *But wait, do I want to solve this so quickly?* I thought. *Can I not buy myself some peace and quiet for this one afternoon—my own hospice for a day?*

I glance over at my own newly wounded car, and I find my hands gripping the spark plug wires as if the group were Sophie's wiggly spine itself. *If I yank these out and snap the distributor cap, not only would the streets be safe from this nearly blind freewheeling terror, but I'd be safe from Sophie's shrieks.*

"Where are you heading off to?" I asked, with the restraint of Gandhi.

"The nursing home on Third and La Jolla, Sharon Care," she answered.

"Oh yeah?" I joked through my anger, "Do they take cars, too?"

"Oh no, does my little Honda need a doctor?"

This poor, purple, long-suffering, shriveled-up Honda Civic, Sheriff—if it were a boxer, it's the Tex Cobb of the auto world, beaten and bloodied after fifteen rounds with this elderly undefeated champ behind the wheel. Some friend had willed it to her, still in immaculate condition, a couple years ago. It now has dents and scratches 360 degrees around, duct tape holding the front lights onto the body, and a twisted coat hanger keeping the rear bumper from jumping free. She scrapes the car along the concrete wall as a guide to get down our driveway, and there's clear evidence, in the form of paint streaks all over it, of the colors of the many cars she's struck. It's like a Jackson Pollock entry in a demolition derby.

With my hands still on the wires, "It might need a doctor," I said. "Give me a minute here." *The hospice patients will just have to hold on for one more day,* I thought. *Sweet mercy, let me do it. Great Red Dragon, Tempter of the Meek, come to me and let me be the absolute destroyer of this engine. Pull, Richard, do it! Pull! Take your revenge!*

"I have a seventeen-year-old girl there who's in her last weeks with AIDS, poor thing," she explained.

My hands sprung off the wires.

"She wants her baby daughter to go to her grandmother, rather than to her rat of an ex-boyfriend who's the father. It's so sad. I'm giving her legal advice for her will."

Damn it. I'm not a terrible person, Sheriff. I got my jumper cables and defibrillated her Civic. And off they both went.

November 8, 4:20 PM

Got home from Target, my last $62.40. Friday afternoon. I'm wiped out. Haven't seen Roxy for days. Says her stomach is still bothering her. I could hear Sophie going before I'd even put my key in the lock. I yelled, "Shut up! Shut up!" standing there outside shouting to nowhere. Then I noticed a note on the door from Irene: "Our showers are backed up. My bathroom and bedroom are flooded again. I called Randall, but will you call him also, please? I can't wash my hair. I should sue him, the bastard. And also, please don't shower until it's fixed, or my place will continue flooding."

Our drains marry into one old pipe underground. It backs up about once a year, and we simultaneously get gunk on our shower and bathroom floors. Her side deservedly gets the worst of it. Sad timing that this is the day of the year that she washes her hair. I called Randall, and he said that he couldn't get his plumber here until Monday. In other words, he's too cheap to pay a weekend rate. "Would you mind terribly using the bath till then?" he chirped. Roxy's a big bath person. I love to see her in there, suds up to her shoulders, knees poking out above the surface. Not for me, though. The dirty water makes no sense, and aromatherapy is an expensive myth. Plus, now I have power, Sheriff—the shower power. Confession: I've done this before—I take a "trickle" when this happens. That's the way my dad always showered—a "trickle"—to save on the water bill. Sometimes he'd come into the bathroom while you were showering, reach behind the curtain, and, with one quick twist, turn the water pressure down and grunt, "Water!"

Irene always says, "Your shower is flooding into my bedroom."

Isn't that too bad? I'm glad to know it's making a mess for her and her dogs. Maybe the overflow will accidentally bathe them all. You know what? Sophie barks—I trickle. That's right, Sheriff. Bark—trickle—bark—trickle. It's ecstasy to me.

11:00 PM

I lost my health insurance today, grace period expired. Can't swing it anymore. If Roxy and I could get married, I'd be on her plan. I'd have more cash to throw at my debt. Teamwork. I'm thinking about getting a medical marijuana license. I have every reason to, except I don't like pot, but maybe it'd help. I have a stabbing pain in my left shoulder and chest. Is this a heart attack?

November 11, 11:30 AM

My nutty sister says to me this morning, "I think you're the one receiving karmic payback."

"So this is my fault? That's what you're suggesting?"

"Not necessarily, but—first, Richard, you need to be more proactive about your life. You see life as things happening to you. Not good."

"Things aren't happening to me?"

"Yes, but you can make proactive choices in your current moments to protect yourself from future karmic redress," she says as if it's given fact.

"So everyone has to be perfect, always, to avoid any pain or payback?"

"Oh, come on," she says. "That's not possible, you know that. This is all part of being a human animal. Ebbs and flows."

"What about Irene's karma then? She's horrible."

"She's an unfortunate woman in an unfortunate period, which may come back to her in her next life or thereafter, or it's boomeranging back now from a different time before."

"She does hospice visits."

"She does? Well, there you go—proactive. She'll be fine."

"Don't my school teaching days count for some karma?"

"That feels like a former you at this point. Calm down and try to understand what you can do in the here and now."

"So, all the crappy things 'here and now' are my doing or my not doing? I'm totally confused."

"I know you won't do acupuncture, but you should at least go get a massage, get your qi unstagnated and moving into a positive flow."

"I don't like strangers touching me."

"That's anxiety, too."

"Ally—you're nuts, but I love you."

"That's good karma, see? More of that. But you're way more nuts."

You don't buy any of her BS, do you, Sheriff? Karma. At this point, I don't even think I could get a self-fulfilling prophecy to come true.

4:00 PM
Plumber was here. No more trickle. Until next time . . .

November 19, 11:30 AM
Took a few days off from the log. Suppose I shouldn't have. Sorry. Depressed. Sophie's been barking all these days, in case you're wondering. Still haven't gotten paid for that *True West* design job. I only charged $300. I've written them two times about it. I also have some weird rash of tiny red blisters in lines going down my left arm. Burns like lit fuses. I can't even get shirt sleeves on, and it's freezing in here.

November 20, 5:30 PM
At the grocery store I got three calls from Casino but no messages. I figured he'd just wanted to borrow a parking pass or something. But when I got back on Hayworth, there were four fire trucks in the middle

of the street. They'd just put out a fire at the building next to ours. A city crew was high up in a cherry picker working on a huge tree that'd been damaged. Everyone jumped back as a big branch came crashing down because they'd fucked up somehow. Luckily it landed in the grass in front of the neighbor's building. That tree is so old and dried out. I never even look up at it, never even think about it. Strange to see a piece of it lying there. I asked Casino why he hadn't left me a message, since our places might have burned to the ground and all. "Oh, I had a lot of calls to make," he said. "I hate waiting for the message and the beep."

Sorry for the inconvenience.

Irene's eyes were alert as the reflection of the spinning red lights pulsed across the thin, translucent skin of her face. Her kitchen windows had been cracked by the heat. "They said the flames were licking the trees over our building. The firemen didn't want to let me go back inside to get my dogs." She handed me a key. "Here. If there's a fire again, will you please go in and get Sophie and Nelson for me? I couldn't live without them."

The sound of a chainsaw shot through the haze. I don't want Irene's key. *I don't want to rescue her dogs. I don't want to die rescuing her dogs.*

"OK," I said. "I'm sure it won't be necessary though." I took the key and put it in my pocket. "Maybe you should teach Nelson how to work a fire extinguisher, just in case."

"Poor Nelson can't even bark if he smells smoke," she said.

That's what's going to happen, Sheriff—there'll be a fire, and Sophie will pull me down with her into eternal perdition engulfed by actual flames.

10:30 PM

It feels like everything is squeezing in on me. I'm getting night sweats. Every night now around 3:00 AM, the start of the witching hour, I wake up in a pool of my own thoughts. It's not enough that my arm is killing me. My sheets are soaked, my hair, my pillow. It's sleep without rest.

In a few hours, it's the four-year anniversary of the morning my mom died, back in Pennsylvania. That afternoon, I remember I got the most wonderful hug from Irene—a long and warm embrace that calmed me, contained me, and gave me a needed pause. She patted me on the back and told me that she was sure that my mom loved me very much. Before that I hadn't realized that they, Irene and my mom, are two similar women, physically—their soft, older, round shape and stature. Irene felt like my mom in my arms. She gave me something that I didn't know I needed or had on a very, very difficult day. I can't believe I'm thinking of that now.

November 23, 1:00 PM

It's over! It's OVER!—OVER!!—I'm actually happy! Remember Scrooge in the last scene of *A Christmas Carol*? Well, Sheriff, I'm telling you right now to please go out and buy us the fattest, sweetest, greasiest, most gluttonous goose you can find! It's time to celebrate!

I saw Irene by her front door this morning and said hello, before I saw what might have been a tear on her cheek. Then, "Do you have any plans for Thanksgiving?" I said, accidentally stepping into whatever cloudy reasons old people have for being weepy around holidays.

"Sophie died today," she said, with the naive expectation of sympathy from me.

Alas, Sophie has finally gone to hell in her very own handbasket, I thought. "What? Dead? She's . . . gone? Are you . . . sure?" I asked, needing absolute, indisputable, incontrovertible confirmation.

"Yes, I put her in my freezer until I can afford to have her cremated."

Confirmation enough. And creepy enough. You mean this is not going to be another "winter of my discontent"? My heart leapt with joy and release, the level of which could only be understood by Nelson Mandela. *We should have her cremated right away,* I thought. *What if she could be unfrozen one day like Walt Disney?*

And there, just as the weight of the world had been unlatched from my yoke, Irene whispered a tearful, faltering, "I'm heartbroken."

Somehow, this evil woman and her evil dog were able to form a malevolent bond that led to something akin to emotions, evil ones.

Only they could have loved one another. Unfortunately, none of the joy in my heart could be used to support her recovery. I gave her a moment of quiet while I wrestled with the image of the dead Sophie coolly petrifying in the freezer, her unblinking eyes ablaze, mouth open, fangs out, tongue curled in a final roar of unstoppable rage at a world that had made her what she was. *On to your next incarnation, you bloodless wretch*, I thought.

"Well—how much do cremations cost?" I asked. "Maybe you should take her to the vet—"

"I have all of my dogs cremated. I like to keep their ashes."

Sophie's ashes wouldn't amount to more than a thimbleful, I calculated.

"I'll be able to do it when my next check comes," she said.

I hope those checks come frequently.

"There's no other food in your freezer, right?" I stammered, staggered by the image of Sophie's freezing corpse, stalactites of dripping, icy rancor forming below her foaming mouth. "Is it OK to have her in there?" I hated myself for this flash of pragmatism, because I'd asked a question that I didn't want answered.

"It's all right," she said.

Not sure how to interpret that, I decided to leave awful enough alone. "Well, I'm, uh . . . I'm sorry about—about Sophie," I said with the sincerity of a blackjack dealer scooping up someone's chips.

"Thank you. She was such a wonderful dog," she said. "I'm going to miss her so much." And with that, she turned to go into her apartment, now left with just the one mute dog, Nelson, and nothing to do but think about the loss of Sophie and to tend to her icy, makeshift morgue.

2:00 PM

I called Roxy to come over and celebrate. I picked up some champagne, and we raised a glass to the deceased Barking Yorkie of North Hayworth Avenue and her quick transfer into the netherworld: *May she, at long last, rest in PEACE. A worthy foe you were, you miserable little bitch.*

Roxy said, "It's so nice to see you smiling." She kissed me. It was warm and slow. Then her leg peeked out from the slit in her skirt and wrapped around mine. Her legs are my weakness. She stayed the night. It was so good to have her here. She had to scramble in the morning for a yoga class.

November 24, 9:00 AM

Is this the end of the log? I guess it is. I certainly won't be needing it. A fitting finish: Sophie dies, and I don't even turn it in. It evaporates into space and time, and all things go back to as they were. Of all the large and wondrous things for which I've worked and prayed—*this is the one that comes true?* Sophie's gone.

This is odd. It's great, but . . . sitting at my desk, there's quiet at the wall where Sophie sounds should be bouncing through. No, I don't miss her. But every time I jump for joy, I land in the freshly dug grave of Irene's bleeding portrait of misery. Sophie was the fulcrum of happiness and anguish between Irene and me. When she was alive, Sophie contented Irene while she was destroying me, and now that she's gone, that's turned around. Irene still has Nelson the Mute; maybe she'll give her attention to him. Two dogs had proven more than she could handle. Long live Nelson.

4:00 PM

This really is it, isn't it? Funny, the deputy said it might not need to go six months. And at least one problem of mine was solved, though I didn't really solve it, nor did this log, because unbeknownst to us, Sophie's barks were numbered. Karma? Maybe my negative energy killed her, so it was a productive suffering. I'll accept congratulations.

The toughest part is saying good-bye to you, Sheriff. It's been so helpful not having this voice clamped up inside my own head but to speak to someone real about it. Well, you're real and not. Some real person would have read this, might have. I have no idea who you are, yet you helped me. For that I thank you sincerely, and I wish you nothing but the best. Be safe.

November 27, 11:30 PM

Fuck the silence. Fuck this solitary confinement. I have a confession: Roxy actually broke up with me two months ago. The things I said about her being here—she wasn't. Not at that time at least. But those were conversations we'd had, moments that are still bouncing around in my head. I'm sorry. She didn't come here the night Sophie died. We didn't drink champagne and kiss. I guess I was dreaming out loud. I almost ripped that page out of this log. I feel pathetic—pretending I wasn't alone, trying to paint a picture of my life that was better than it is. But it's not. And now I'm tortured by the quiet, this new absence of everything. So I'm in this log again, which no one will read. I'd actually started this thing as a way to try to solve one of my life's many problems. But it hasn't helped, really. And why should I have mentioned to you that I was so sad? It didn't seem relevant. But I can't stop thinking about her.

What happened was she'd called and said she wanted to talk, but when she got here she just ended it. Seven years. She'd brought my stuff over in two bags and set them down by the door. I saw them and, like a fool, only thought she'd been shopping. But most of my belongings from her place were in there. Breakup bags. Instant. She was done. Her face was a death mask.

"I feel like this isn't going anywhere anymore," she said.

"Of course it is. It's right here. We have—"

"No, you don't seem to want any more than this. You've drifted out to sea with no way back."

"You're my. . . . We're looking at apartments. We have a whole list."

"We haven't looked for five weeks. You don't even realize it. And you're right, we were looking *at* apartments, not *for* an apartment. You're never going to fully commit to anything in your life, are you?" she said. "You have to get your shit together."

I floundered through explanations, but I had no evidence that would hold. I moved out here to be a musician, and that didn't take. Left teaching. Ended up in debt. Now everything is over. Except,

Sheriff, that her last words to me as she was getting into her car were "I love you, Richard."

I said, "I love you, too. That's why I want us to work on this." I pleaded for time, a chance. But she buckled up, looked at me, forced a slight smile on her lips, then turned the ignition and drove off. Her eyes are so beautiful, even when I think about that moment. My head is still spinning about it. I do think she loves me. I do. But I also think that she can't love me because of who I've turned out to be. Look at the weak, angry bozo in this log, for Pete's sake. We haven't spoken since.

"You have to get your shit together." I can't shake that because it sounds so solvable, as in if she sees my shit together, she'll come back, right? So stupid—I thought if I could get the dog to stop barking, I could prove something. I wonder if Roxy somehow got a look at my Chase credit card statement. I don't think she knows how often I've had to use it to live off of recently. It's rough just finding a way to make the minimum payment, hovering near $500 a month like a drone circling a terrorist. I don't know.

November 28, 3:45 PM

This afternoon I saw Irene standing at the end of the driveway, her head drooped toward the sidewalk, her eyes seeming to stare through the concrete toward the secrets of the spinning earth. Nelson the Mute was lying there at the end of his rope, now a lone dog, panting in the hot sun, which gave his body comfort on the warm stone. Irene's arms were fallen and empty, defeated by the heavy despair of loss. I watched her from behind my screen door. I'd gasped for air while struggling to be silent, and a tear dampened my eye. Everything that was sad about her was sad about me—her Sophie, my Roxy—trying to understand why things end, how they end, how joy can be so here but must be so temporary, always, or it would be unrecognizable. I stepped outside. "Hi, Irene, how are you doing today, a little better?"

"Terrible." Nelson got up from his lounging spot.

"Nelson is here," I said. "He seems like a good boy."

"Nelson is my entire heart and soul," she said. "He's everything to me. He doesn't like being alone now."

I walked toward them, and Nelson tried to bark. He does the whole motion of a bark, like he's trying to chomp on an invisible hamburger that's hovering like the fruit of Tantalus just above his head—but no bark, only a pale sound as if he's clearing his throat through his nose. It's actually kind of cute—only because it's nearly inaudible.

Irene wore her grief more sadly than her stained housedress. It'll take some time to wash them both out.

"Where's Roxy?" she asked. "I haven't seen her car around."

I almost said, "She's buried in my freezer until I can save enough money to have her cremated," but laughter was an entire solar system away. "She's not around right now" was all I mumbled. If I'd explained any more of our situation, I'd be staring at the sidewalk just like Irene.

"Oh, I won't ask," she said, after having asked.

"Thank you. I don't know what's going to happen, so it's not worth talking about right now."

"I understand about relationships," she said. Nelson had settled back by now. I reached down to pat him on the head, but his horrifying hair of encrusted crud kept me from going all the way. I smiled and came back inside. Maybe she'd only wanted to deflect her mind into someone else's sadness for a moment, but we'd had an actual conversation there—absent of conflict.

9:20 PM

Today was Thanksgiving, by the way. I didn't go anywhere. Don't want anyone sitting next to me but Roxy. Thanksgiving was the first holiday we'd spent together. She told me later on that she'd been watching me from across the kitchen that day, and she'd caught herself thinking, *That is my husband standing there.*

All I have right now is this journal.

I did do charity once. I helped deliver Thanksgiving meals to poor families around my hometown, Wilkes-Barre, Pennsylvania, as part of my duties as sophomore class president at Bishop Hoban. Four of us climbed into the green and gold school van with feisty Sister Bernardo, and she drove us around to the poorest neighborhoods. I felt like Robert Kennedy. A lot of these people lived in shanty trailers at the foot of the Pocono Mountains. I'd no idea that there were so many destitute people. Wilkes-Barre had been on its knees for many years as anthracite coal, its main industry, had died decades before and nothing replaced it but the many tall, barren, rolling dunes of culm—the black, useless waste grains left over from mining. Streets were even paved through those gigantic culm banks like lifeless mountain passes on a dusty black planet. There's something about a smaller town that makes you think that no one can hide. People surviving on welfare checks. My parents bitched about the "welfares" all the time. My mother once took a Polaroid of a neighbor mowing his own grass and sent it to President Carter as proof the guy could work. But often, when we were out of the van and had gotten the people to open their doors, we were greeted with tears. Food can make people cry.

I didn't hear Irene leave at all today. I wonder if she had no Thanksgiving to go to, or if hospice was closed or something. It's hard to know when Irene comes and goes now without Sophie barking about it. What a sad state we're all in—on a day for giving thanks . . . for what? It was all about dreams when I first came here, escaping, building something, but now I'm long past the chance. Los Angeles has a way of letting you know.

I admit it, I wanted to be a rock star, Sheriff. I have to laugh, now that I'm pushing forty and nearly twenty pounds overweight. As the years have gone by, I've seen real dreams of real friends come true. I know that it does work sometimes. My friend Nick has become a very successful actor in commercials and TV. He now has a beautiful little house in North Hollywood with a great wife and two kids. My friend Dan was a stand-up comedian, and not a great one, just loud. *Dudes do this! Chicks do that!, blah, blah* . . .—ugh—but he got a gig writing on *Penny's Play Date*, a kids' show, for God's sake, and now he has a two-bedroom condo in Reseda and a new used Harley. It can work.

I got close, but it just didn't happen for me. I used to have great stuff. When I first came to town, I could teach during the day, and write or record or play out at night. A perfect plan. I'd never be a destitute songwriter living on people's sofas. I'd have a benefits package and a great story for interviews. "Teachin' and rockin'—rockin' and teachin'," I used to say.

That's the guy Roxy fell in love with. I was working on my album in a studio in Hermosa Beach, making plans for a possible small West Coast tour. The album was taking forever, and would take much longer than that. I was in my sixth year teaching at Crenshaw High when Roxy arrived there as a counselor. She'd graduated from UC Davis and spent two years working at a junior high. Out to save the world. She has straight shoulder-length hair, a midnight black that shined like the onyx of Cleopatra, pulled back in a tight ponytail to cover her flowing youth with seriousness and efficiency. I melted like a nickel in a foundry when I saw her. We'd assembled in the library on the morning of the teachers' in-service, the day before the first day of classes in late August. All the sullen, coffee-sipping teachers' faces glistened with frustrated sweat, because the district refused to turn on the air-conditioning with no students in attendance. But Roxy was cool, her stunning blue eyes shimmering like a refreshing backyard pool.

She introduced herself. "I'm replacing Mr. Burke in our diligent team of three," she said. There was a startlingly sexy slight British accent. (Her mom was born in Canterbury; she's half English and half Russian.) "My areas of concentration are identifying at-risk students and organizing outreach programs for families in need of bridging the gap between home and school."

"They're all at risk," Mr. Monroe, next to me, whispered.

"Shut the fuck up, you cynical, old windbag fuck," I said out of the side of my mouth. I felt like punching him in his pleats for disturbing the reminder of the virgin idealism we'd each once possessed. She was a young robin singing in the morning sunshine. Love had conquered me already, and we hadn't even gotten to the faculty team-building exercises yet.

We met for drinks and jazz on the patio at the Cat 'n' Fiddle on Sunset that very night. Our first year together was amazing. Roxy loved everything about her "domesticated rock star . . . you're a snapshot of masculine duality, a modern Dionysus," she'd tease me over her pinot noir, "the rebellious artist yet conforming caretaker." She used to joke that I had "bipolar professional disorder." "How many other budding rock stars have a college degree and health insurance?" But she also had two sides, working that soft hair, the bright red lips, and that little ass in a short skirt plenty at my gigs, make no mistake. My Persephone—goddess of Hades, goddess of spring growth.

I recorded just the one album—*L.A. Never Dies*, it was called. I loved this city, even with its inherent contradictions. I wrote the lyrics to the title track during the riots. Two of the songs are about Roxy. By that time I'd been through three different managers: one who only wanted to translate my songs and sell them to singers in Eastern Europe, one who tried to lure me into the Church of Scientology, and one who gave the weekend manager at Luna Park a hand job under the table—while I was stuck there dumbfounded—so I could get a Saturday-night gig. Not the most powerful players.

I taught myself web and design skills when I decided to leave teaching, because the work could be flexible and at home. That way I could play more gigs here and overnights out of town, for what my managers could get me.

Almost a third of us at Crenshaw High were young and inexperienced. They nicknamed the five of us new, white male teachers "the Osmond Brothers." Every faculty member faced challenge after challenge with the kids. I had to send one of my students, Monique, to Roxy because she'd told me about her plan to shoot her mother in the face when she got home. They found the gun under her bed exactly as she'd described. Her mother had a revolving door of men, drugs, and alcohol, and was forcing Monique into their sexual circus. Roxy helped get her into foster care and worked with her throughout that year. Another of my students, Dae-Ho, when I'd kept him after class to ask about why he hadn't had his reading exercises book for three straight days, begged me not to call his home about it and then lifted his shirt, revealing crisscrossed welts on his back from his collar to his waist. His alcoholic uncle/caretaker had beaten him with a golf club for breaking a dish. Roxy got him out that night with the help of Child Services. She was such strength for the kids. But it was tough to bear sometimes—endless gang activity, so many students so many years behind grade level, countless dysfunctional and danger-ous homes for her "outreach." A lot of hard hours, breaking points, but we rode the monster waves and managed to laugh and drink together, allowing ourselves some avoidance in each other's arms.

Even though I was young, I had a pretty good sense of authority with the kids. One of my tricks was to have them stand outside of the classroom, single file along the lockers until they could achieve complete silence, as a unit, for sixty seconds straight before being allowed to come into the room. It was about respecting the space and one another. They complained, banged on lockers, threatened me. But they eventually progressed to lining up quietly with a sense of pride and ownership of what was rightfully theirs.

Roxy and I endlessly debated my brilliant methodology. "You're minimizing their growing sense of authority within themselves by overreaching your own," she'd say.

"I am the only authority in the classroom."

"Yes, but young adolescents need to experience their natural progression toward adulthood, and you're still treating them like children."

"I'm getting them to act like adults more quickly than anybody else."

"Mr. Mesa's going to have a talk with you about it very soon, I bet."

"That's fine. Whenever he does, I'll ask him if he thinks that these ninth graders in South Los Angeles, reading at a fourth-grade level—at best—are really itching to read *The Call of the Wild*, which is what's next up. They don't give a fuck about a dogsled team car-rying mail across the Klondike. I'm going to make it a team effort, so they understand that learning for themselves is important, but others learning equally around them is just as important for the community and for society."

"OK, Buck."

"Hmmm. Sarcasm is the intellectual white flag."

"You're not impressed that I remembered the name of the dog from *The Call of the Wild?*"

"I'd be more impressed if you agreed with me."

"You're out on the Klondike with that fantasy, poor thing. Is it cold way out there—so all alone?"

This shit might make your stomach turn, Sheriff, but you have no idea how much I miss it. How can she not miss it? I want to call her, but I can't.

Anyhow, happy Thanksgiving. I guess I shouldn't be keeping this log anymore now that Sophie's thawing in the nether regions, so this is also "so long." And thank you.

December

December 12, 10:20 AM

Only two weeks have passed, and you're not going to believe this:
Irene has a new dog, and it's another fucking Yorkie—and it barks!
She got it for herself as an early Christmas present—"to beat the rush."
Do people actually give Yorkshire terriers to other people as *presents*?

It had been here for a week—and barking—but I hadn't seen it
yet, because I was laid up with the flu. When I finally went outside
and caught them on a walk, I asked, "What is this, Irene? Are you
babysitting?"

"Meet Lauren," she smiled. "Lauren Bacall. She was already named that. I just got her. Isn't she gorgeous? Don't you just love her tail?"

"*Bark. Bark, bark, bark,*" Lauren interrupted.

What have I done to deserve this cursed life?

Lauren is younger than Sophie was—but bigger, stronger, louder, and already mangy looking.

"She's a Yorkie, and she barks. You're not going to keep her, Irene?" I implored. "We've been through this."

"She's just nervous. Excited to meet you. Say hi to Richard, Lauren."

Lauren said hi, all right. She wouldn't shut up with saying hi, displaying with great enthusiasm the full-throated vigor of youth. It gave me a cramp in my neck. *She'll be around for years*, I thought. *What a selfish—*

"Don't you love her gray hair? That's a sign of pedigree. It crushed me when Nelson's hair went blond," Irene said.

Lauren's bushy tail spun in a blur of raw energy that could power four city blocks. For a moment, she stopped barking and looked at me. Her eyes were young, wide, and innocent like a rabbit's. *This one's a manipulator.* "She's not going to bark uncontrollably though," I warned. "Right?"

"Oh, she'll be all right. You're so uptight. She's just a little dog," she snorted, "and I need to feel safe."

Lauren stood there panting, overheated already from the cardio of the full-body barking and that thick hair insulating her like a space suit. Nelson the Mute chewed on weeds in the cracks of the sidewalk. Off on his own, he seemed indifferent, an aloof Bogie to his new Bacall.

"Keep your windows locked, don't open your door to strangers, and you'll be safe," I directed. But my speech fell on a deaf ear. There's a new dog in town, Sheriff. I have a bad feeling.

11:15 PM

Just a note: it was my birthday on December 7, while I was fighting off the flu and blissfully unaware that the respite that followed

Sophie's death was officially over. It was a hard one. I got a few texts from friends, but I didn't want to be around anyone. I did get a funny text from Ally saying, "Happy birthday from the Ghost of Sophie—arf arf." And Roxy sent me one: "Wishing you a happy birthday. Have a great one!" How fucking restrained—and generic—is that? Why even fucking bother? Except she did think of me. I don't know. It was just obligatory bullshit, right?

December 13, 1:00 PM

Yep—Lauren's a barker. Holy shit, she's as aggressive as a razorback. Barks at anything that moves.

How long do Yorkies live? For that matter—how long do decrepit old ladies live? Is Irene just fucking with me? Did Lauren's dog pen have a sign on it that read ESPECIALLY LOUD?

I have a question, Sheriff: I can just continue with this log where it left off, right? I shouldn't have to start over just because it's a different dog. It's the same owner, same address, same breed for damn sake. I've been continuing it anyway. It wouldn't be fair to make me begin again. I can't. I won't. I've put in my time. Please let all those weeks with Sophie count toward something, or I'll fall apart.

December 15, 9:15 AM

I've given up. Depression is an inertia, an emotional numbness that spreads over your body through the painful decay of being who you are, and everything that's been hurtful in your life is evidence of all the hurt that's sure to come. Now this. I've already started walking over to Irene's door to yell at Lauren. I know Irene's home, but she doesn't react. Lauren just barks back at me. Nelson jumps up and down and chomps at the invisible hamburger. I hate them all. I'm staying in bed today.

December 19, 9:15 AM

Still not over the flu. Got an e-mail from that client who'd called me at the café. They're officially "moving on," going "in-house," which amazes me because it's more expensive to hire someone full-time. Anyhow, usually clients just disappear, so at least they sent me a disappointment note.

Not a great day for the inbox. Also got a "How are you doing?" e-mail from Roxy out of the blue. As much as I'd wanted to hear from her, I didn't anticipate this generic crap. Very distant. Condescending, too. *How am I doing?* If not "well," then what would she do about it? I'm not doing well, and it's greatly because of her. She's menacing me with a random shot like that. She's obviously thinking about me, but it's from residual guilt because she left. I don't care how her conscience feels. I don't want her remorse. I want her. I miss everything. But maybe I'm wrong. Maybe she misses me a little.

I'm jealous of the world, because every single man on the planet has a chance at her now—except me. I've gained seven pounds since Lauren showed up. Yorkie weight. My face is breaking out. I can't let Roxy see me. Why bother cleaning the peanut butter off my hands when I'm just going to get more on them in a minute? Life is simpler this way. Crunchy Cheetos. Trader Joe's red wine in a box. Everyone just go away.

December 21, 10:15 AM

I just stepped out to see if Irene was home so I could complain to her about Lauren. No answer. I walked around back to see if her car was here, but it wasn't. Casino was back there in his section of the garage, which he's converted to a workout room, and on hot days he works out with his area's door open and his shirt conspicuously off. He was spinning slowly on his exercise bike when he saw me. "What's a matter, Richard? Everything OK?"

That's a crappy, judgmental thing to ask. I mentioned Lauren, and Casino spit out his go-to advice: "You've got to drop a dime to Randall." He continued pedaling. "This shit is tearing you apart. Look at yourself. You're white as cream cheese. You've got big circles under your eyes. You look like the Hamburglar. And—you're fat all of a sudden. What have you gained, like, thirty-five pounds? You're single now. This should be the best time of your life. But now you're back here, looking around, trying to see if Irene's home, talking to yourself: 'That goddamned dog. That goddamned little Lauren.' C'mon, man, you need to figure out how to solve your own problems."

He continued with a great deal of unsolicited advice, sitting there, as he was, looking down at me from high atop his exer-cycle. All the while, I was stuck there listening, trying not to tell him to go fuck himself.

"Life's about choices, man. You've got to learn to be happy within yourself. The Dalai Lama said, 'The purpose of our lives is to be happy.' I know Roxy left you and all, but if you continue to be miserable and just let everything around you control your life, you're never going to be happy."

"Yeah, you're right, Casino." What else could I say? I was choking back a vomit of grief at the mention of Roxy's name.

"You ought to get out and see some girls. That's what you need. See some ass. Be reminded how crowded the ocean is. Give some skirt a nice, cold uppercut. I'm going to be at Lola's tonight around ten thirty. My buddy Brooklyn is tending bar. We'll hook you up."

"What does the Dalai Lama say about uppercuts?"

"He has his happy. I have mine."

I have none.

Then he generously added, "The ladies need to be happy, too." With that, his pedaling picked up speed, and I slunk back under my exer-rock.

December 25, 1:00 PM

Santa brought me barking for Christmas. Drinking Jack Daniel's so it won't feel like a holiday. Work for yourself you don't get holidays anyhow. Live next to a horror-dog, you don't get holidays. God . . . Christmas. Roxy.

4:45 PM

My neighbor Stasya saved me again. She's seen me many times in the evenings when I step outside, either fuming because of Sophie or Lauren or now suffocating from solitude. She stands in the driveway next to the shrubs, wearing her Dodger blue housecoat and slippers, smoking Virginia Slims. Midsixties. She's from Russia and carries the intensity of escaping Communism in her ever-squinting, musty gray eyes. She's proud. She's five feet tall and has the hearty, low-weighted stature of a corner mailbox. She steps outside to smoke, she says, because her husband has emphysema. "My poor Nikolai . . ." Marriage is all about compromise.

I enjoy the smell of cigarette smoke, and I enjoy Stasya. In the beginning, she used to only watch me in contemplative silence, one eyebrow raised over the long, thin, glowing cigarette. I could sense her worry for me, as if she were helping to breathe in my anger, hold it, and then exhale it away forever into the speechless night air.

But now we talk. She's insecure about her English, so she speaks in careful, short phrases, three or four words at a time, but the philosophical weight of her thoughts manifests itself as with the restrained touch of a thundering poet. She liked Roxy. Since Roxy is half Russian, they occasionally shared a Virginia Slim and chatted in Russian. She likes to talk to me about her. And she smiles. Though her teeth have been decimated from decades of Soviet-era dentistry and tobacco, it's a beautiful smile to me. The embers of her cigarette reflect in her eyes, and they sparkle with hope.

Tonight, she reassured me—on Christmas day. "You are the man."

"Yes, but—"

"My Richard, you have the power," she said, touching my arm, smiling.

"I don't know what to do. Time's going by."

"You don't have to do anything," she insisted. "Love is love. It does not break. She needs to think. And she loves you. I know this in my heart."

I pray that Roxy's Russian side feels these things.

"Does she love me enough that one day she'll smoke outside if I need an oxygen tent?" Stasya laughs. I guess living the bulk of one's life under tyrannical oppression gives a person a decent sense of humor. Her finger brushes the hair behind my ear. The touch of a woman's hand is a smooth tranquilizer, even when it comes from the outstretched arm of a cigarette-smoking mailbox.

These conversations always do me good. "Love is love. It does not break." She occasionally speaks in Russian to me, and though I don't understand a word, it makes these moments seem as timeless as the stars. I now go toward the incense of Virginia Slims like a moth to a Goodwill bin. Stasya gives me hope and strength about love's endurance. But I don't know if she's a shepherd or a Judas goat.

10:00 PM

My arm is still killing me—this rash or whatever keeps growing. Ally says I've got shingles, like an old person. She says it's from stress, like an old person. Ibuprofen isn't even touching it, like it wouldn't for an old person. I should get that medical marijuana. Ally's against it, believe it or not. "'Altering' your mind isn't 'changing' your mind," she says. "That's what you've got to work on. You should try Tai Chi."

"My knee won't let me stand on one leg. They seem to do that a lot."

"It's low impact, and it would help you with everything, even Irene."

"I'd have to be Tai Chi–ing all day long. Irene's the one who should be doing Tai Chi for her balance."

"Getting shingles at your age doesn't prove anything to you?"

"Yes, chicken pox sucks. We should eradicate it. I'm going to dedicate my life to that."

She's overnighting me some "colloidal silver, proteolytic enzymes, and olive leaf extract" to rub on it. Oh boy.

I'm trying to write a response e-mail to Roxy. I want to tell her that I want to talk, that I'd listen to everything she has to say, and that I can change. But I'd said all that already, in pieces, on the day of the Breakup Bags. Do you think I even should e-mail her? Plus, so far, I have no changes to talk about, except that I've gotten rid of my wallet chain, and that I'm doing pour-over coffee since my machine broke. The problem is I want to say too much, and it's radioactively pathetic—and how embarrassing to be back at square one with a worse dog next door? I don't know if there's another man. I don't know if she thinks about me. I don't know if she's angry that I haven't reached out to her enough. I'm scared of everything. Why'd she tell me she loved me that day?

This is all getting to be too much. I cry about it, or everything, just about every day, to be honest, Sheriff. Every day around this time. If not cry, I at least collapse on the couch, defeated. I just haven't been mentioning it. I think it's sundowners, i.e., depression. Old people get it when the natural sunlight dissolves at the end of each day. This is when I start drinking. Now. It helps. I can't get her off my mind, and the evenings tide in with insecurity and longing because it's social time, especially Fridays and Saturdays—and Sundays. Damn, we loved watching the Steelers on Sundays. Even being together on any weeknight means dinner and wine.

I'm crippled. Plus Lauren. My friends still hang out with Roxy sometimes. I hate feeling "betrayed," because we're all adults, and people make choices, and there should be no sides, but I do feel it, even though I know it's selfish and irrational. I don't know what she's doing, but she's single, right? Why wouldn't she be out there having fun by now, making herself available? And it's the holidays—no one wants to be alone. It's her right, and my friends' rights, and my shit's not together. I can't just snap my fingers. I hate the sunset. Alcohol keeps the light at least one finger above the horizon.

I feel like I'm in the psych ward at the downtown jail. I told you I've been there. Maybe I saw you when I was there? Did you know the chaplain, Father Will? I knew him because he also taught a few history classes at Crenshaw. He'd wanted the jail job, and he said he'd been a shoo-in because he was an African American Catholic priest, something "all too rare" in Southern California. He liked my songs. He thought I'd find my "Johnny Cash moment" if I spoke with some inmates. I went with him six times. One time we went into the psych ward of the "hospital" wing. Have you been there? The din of screaming—a haunted, indiscernible language of pleading madness—agitated my every atom, with smell and taste already struggling in my stomach all morning. We approached a cell door and were confronted by a loud, color-coded sticker: DANGER TO CARETAKERS. DANGER TO SELF. FECAL/URINE/SPIT/HIV.

Father Will and I hadn't been offered any precautions—no masks, gloves, shields. I didn't say anything. I trusted him. The guard opened the door, and we stepped forward through what may as well have been a gateway back to the middle ages. There was a metal cot with a two-inch-thick foam mattress on which laid a man clothed only in an adult diaper, his ankles each chained to corners of the cot, and his right arm cuffed to the side. Only his left arm was free to move. I'd compare the scene to a beast of burden, but I'd never seen an animal shackled with such extreme. Beads of sweat slid from his limbs, ticking seconds off into puddles on the concrete floor, and he moaned elongated syllables from some anguished conversation in his ghosted mind.

Will knelt at his side and took his hand. "I'm going to pray for you, my son," he said. "What would you like me to say?"

The inmate stared at the ceiling. "I . . . I need to stop jerking myself off," he said. Then his bony hips twisted slightly, and he pulled his diaper away to reveal massively swollen testicles. "I can't stop." His rabid eyes turned toward Will. "I'm . . . I'm . . . hurting myself," and then he went back to mumbling.

Father Will improvised a prayer. I don't know how much of it the inmate heard or understood. Or how much God heard or understood. This is one of his creatures, is he not? Am I not?

December 26, 12:50 PM

Oh, man—bad news. Weird news. I don't know. Irene just fell. I mean a real fall, Sheriff. Outside. I'd just gotten out of the shower when I heard my name called out from the front, "Richard!!" Then "*Ooow . . . Ooh! . . . Help me!*"

I ran outside to see her lying on her back in a patch of grass under the bush next to my steps.

"I think I broke my arm," she moaned.

I thought of my mother as she must have fallen and lost her last breath. "It's going to be OK," I said.

"I can't move."

"You shouldn't move. I'm calling 9-1-1 right now. Lie still."

The paramedics were here in about six minutes. (I'm glad the dispatcher didn't tell me to write a six-month Broken Arm Log.) Irene grew surprisingly calm by the time they were at her side.

A small crowd gathered on the sidewalk, mostly older people from the building next door. Casino and Jazmine came running. Stasya stood by. People are drawn to sirens, witnessing pain, as they need to be reminded of their own limitations.

"What happened to her?" they kept asking me.

"She just fell, that's all," I offered, trying to keep everyone at ease. But falling is a very different accident for someone in their seventies than it is for you or me. Roxy's dad passed away eight weeks after a "he just fell" incident because he contracted an infection that took quick advantage of his old age. It doesn't seem right to "just fall" and then die, as if the earth can suck you into it at will. But I didn't want to worry. This isn't my mother or Roxy's dad. Irene is a foul, angry, selfish human being who has housed the furry bane of my existence for the last three years.

"She was very calm, not complaining," I told the neighbors as the ambulance rolled away. "I think she'll be fine. The paramedics didn't seem overly concerned. She'll be OK." None of them were friendly with Irene. The older neighbors were wanting me to tell them that they'd be fine, too, if they were to fall. It was hope talk.

5:20 PM

I haven't heard anything about Irene yet. It's been five hours. I don't know from whom I would hear. I've never seen anyone come over to visit. Other than the hospice patients, where are her people? Do they know that something's happened? Lauren's barking like a banshee. Nelson is probably manic, too. I wonder when Irene will be sent home? Man, this is weird.

10:00 PM

I wish I could call Roxy, but I can't. I feel like I should tell her about Irene. I miss Roxy. It's bad and terrible. All I think about. The midnight texts. Playing gin rummy until we fell asleep on each other's shoulders, the cards all over the place in the morning. She kept a running tally of our scores in a composition book, months and months and months long. I miss—I apologize, Sheriff, too much wine tonight. I miss running my index finger down the curve of her spine, how she breathes when she sleeps—a single, tiny little snore every three or four minutes. I miss how she slept in little socks and would press her feet against mine until they got warm. I miss gently rubbing ice cubes on her nipples and watching her lose control. Her kisses, so long and soft, and slow. She had a "sexy face" she could make with her eyes during sex that could make me come pretty much whenever she wanted. She's an early riser, and she sometimes used to rub my shoulders for a few seconds before she left the bed. In fact, sometimes my hair gets all matted and wild against the pillow. She's got a whole series of morning-sleep photos of me. She couldn't get enough of laughing at that. I hated it. I miss it now. Damn it. And it's football season. The Steelers are 9-5 and might make the playoffs, and we haven't even talked about it. A girl who loves your teams as much as you do—wears the jerseys—sometimes just with boy shorts, Sheriff. I can't even face Sundays.

It's money, right? She's been working on her master's, eyeing a PhD. Money makes a difference. I'd planned to become filthy rich. Now I pocket my quarters and trudge my drunk ass up to Launderland to wash my fading clothes.

I'm drunk-dog-logging. Dog logging Under the Influence.

I've filled a big box with Roxy's stuff. It's been sitting here like a coffin at a Catholic wake this whole time. I folded everything nicely, included some of her old notes and photos. If she wants total separation, then here it is. I thought of just donating everything, but I can't. Probably should have done this sooner, but I couldn't. I can't stand the box being here. But I can't move myself to send it. I have to put some kind of note in there. Have you ever had to do this? What am I supposed to write?

Here are your things, Roxy, your cosmetics, soaps, pajamas, T-shirts, yoga pants, extra jeans, emergency little black dress, lingerie, fuck-me heels and stockings, our bear, Franklin, your linen pants . . . the rummy book. I miss you. It feels like I'm tearing off my own skin.

That's all I can think of. Feeble—in other words, honest. She knows how I feel. Maybe there's nothing more to the point than silence.

She'll look for a note or a little surprise. I could always make her laugh with some goofy purchase from Big Lots or the 99¢ Store. Maybe what she needs is time with me not being around, not being thought about 24/7. Maybe no message is a good message, a show of self-respectability.

11:55 PM

It's midnight, and I've heard nothing happening next door except Lauren's barking—and now light whimpering. No one's coming to check on the dogs? It's been nine hours.

I have that key to Irene's from the fire. I'm going to go over there, see if they're hungry or anything. Wish me luck.

12:20 AM

Holy shit, I can't believe what I just saw. I'm hardly able to get my breath back from holding it for so long, because the air over there blasted at me like an open furnace of bacteria. It's a filthy madhouse at Irene's. She's a hoarder. I only managed to stay in there for about ninety seconds, but from what I could see—the light is burned out in her front room—it's all junk: bags, magazines, books, newspapers, Tupperware, linens, video cassettes, garbage. The dogs must not be trained at all, because the floors are a sloshy cesspool. I've seen her walk them. I guess not enough. I could find nowhere to step that wasn't trudging through a shallow swamp.

The dogs were penned in the kitchen behind a wrought iron gate. Lauren squealed and squealed at me as if an elephant were kneeling on her neck. Nelson kept leaping against the gate, making it pound against the loose latch like a prisoner's old-time tin cup. Presuming that Irene didn't want the dogs in the living room, I stepped over the gate and into the kitchen hoping to find some food for the two of them, who were now darting around in a panic like loose fireworks.

The floor was damp brown with what looked like mud but smelled of much worse. I kept telling myself it was mud, but I wasn't very convincing. There were wet patches and dry, caked areas. The dogs' hair was matted with having sat in this for so long, as if neither had been bathed since leaving the warm amniotic fluids of their own mothers' wombs.

I couldn't take the smell in that ammonia fog. Having my T-shirt pulled up around my nose was quickly running its course. Finally, among the bags and dishes and containers that covered the counter, I found their dry food, tossed a handful into each bowl, and fled for fresh air through the front door like a rescued miner.

I took off my shoes and left them outside before I came in my place and went straight to a hot shower. I could still hear Lauren barking when I'd come clean. I hope they can settle down for the night. I'm sure that Irene'll be back tomorrow.

2:00 AM

Can't sleep. I'm in shock. Can't get the smell of Irene's out of my sinuses. Is that old age, what I saw next door? Ending up alone, fading into oneself—one's worst self? Letting everything go? She's her own prisoner over there, trapped by her mind the way my father was trapped by his own body after the stroke—just sitting there waiting for the rest of his body to go. At Irene's, the prison will build up around her until she suffocates. And that smell, the smell of death—no, the smell of waiting for death—reminded me of the jail visits. I met Richard Ramirez, the "Night Stalker" serial killer, there, also waiting to die—surrounded by horror, facing death row.

Through the small, thick, scratched, permanently fogged window of his cell door, Father Will introduced us and then politely offered Ramirez a prayer. Ramirez politely refused, and then, with great pride, pointed our eyes toward the large pentagram he'd laid out from wet, rolled-up toilet paper on the floor. Then Ramirez turned to me. "What's it like teaching kids today?" he asked.

"Oh, it's not bad," was all I said. We didn't really hit it off.

Then I witnessed the moment when Father Will offered the promise of forgiveness and redemption through prayer to that man. Amazing. I almost asked Will for a prayer of my own that day. Today's the anniversary of the day my father died. Always a tough day for me. I think about him and me, and forgiveness that I can't give.

I told you he was an alcoholic, a severe man, and my mom had consigned matrimony to acrimony. That was our household. I can't remember a day as a child when I didn't want to be somewhere else, with another family, friends, our hippie neighbors—anyone, anywhere. My best and worst attempt at running away came in the first grade. I'd told my friend Dale about being afraid of my father, being hit with his belt, and together we devised a plan. After school one day, I'd get on Dale's bus, go to his house, and from there he'd walk with me to the Greyhound bus station on the square downtown. Then I'd ride the 120 miles south to Philadelphia. That's where the Liberty Bell was, and I loved the Phillies, so it all made perfect sense.

On that day, I'd packed an extra duffel bag with underwear, a pair of Toughskins, my Steelers pajamas, and a Pink Panther T-shirt that Ally'd given me for my birthday. All progressed without a hitch until our teacher, Miss Lord, approached us in the line for the bus. "Excuse me, Smiley [my nickname then], do you have permission to go on Dale's bus today?" she asked, pointing at my extra bag. "Because I wasn't told."

"Yes." And she didn't stop me. We felt like we were in *Hogan's Heroes*. At Dale's house, we spent an hour in his room figuring out when we should leave. But the sun was going down, and as the aroma of pot roast crept up the stairs, Dale thought he might not be able to go. Then his mom came into the room. "Richard, your father's on his way. You can stay up here until then if you like." Miss Lord had contacted him. Dale and I silently fumbled with his plastic army men while we waited.

Dad looked sharp as ever in his suit from work. He thanked Mrs. Murphy and took me by the arm. I choked down any crying so Dale wouldn't see. On the ride home, Dad yelled, "Where were you going? What were you doing?"

"Philadelphia," I said, and "I don't know why."

The house was empty when we got home. He took me up to his bedroom, tossed me on his bed, and pulled off his belt. His anger must have thrown off his aim because the usual formality of this ritual went haywire. I screamed as he swung and swung. I kicked and squirmed, but his arm controlled me like a metal press. He kept asking why I'd done it. I wasn't smart, or mature, or brave enough to say, "This" and "*YOU.*" I just repeated that "I wanted to go to see the Phillies." I urinated all over myself, him, and the bed. He didn't stop. When he finally released me, he told me to get fresh sheets and clean up. I never ran away again—for fear of failing.

For all these years, I've tried to forget my father's behavior. But I have to figure this out right now, or I'm not going to make it. His father left when he was born. On top of that, when he was five, his mother committed suicide by mercury poisoning. He was the one who found her dead on the kitchen floor. That abandonment is incontrovertibly real. He would never allow anyone to disappear on him again. I sure couldn't.

Sometimes it seems so ridiculous that I can't let go of the dad stuff—and sometimes it feels like everything that I am. And now Roxy's gone, and I'm in a panic. I'm wide awake like a bloodhound. At my father's funeral, the priest asked me to read from Matthew 5:5: "The meek shall inherit the earth." *Really?* I thought. I was bitter— for myself and for my father. He'd inherited nothing but pain and confusion, and he'd passed it on to me. What am I supposed to do with it? What am I supposed to do with Irene's?

Do you believe in redemption, Sheriff? Does Roxy? Does Irene? Do I?

I can't become him. Maybe instead of ignoring it, if I figure him out, I can get somewhere. The best I can see it, his anger was forged by a paradoxical mixture of ego and self-loathing. He always felt that he wasn't getting what he deserved in life, yet he hated himself for his own lack of achievement. Yes, he was rough on me, but he wasn't *all* bad. He also made every concert at school, etc. And he had a happy drunk side. He could be an awesome drunk, funny, caring, hand-on-your-shoulder, partner-with-you-in-the-egg-toss-at-the-Bowlers-Picnic dad. You always think that good side will stay. It doesn't. You try to cajole it back by laughing around him when you're sad or smiling when you're afraid, like when he throws up on himself next to you in the backseat of the car on the way home from that same Bowlers Picnic.

Were his unresolved frustrations passed down to me? Have I been avoiding some cosmic pathway of trying to make them right?

After his birth parents were gone, he got a new life through adoption. He was so reticent to talk about his early childhood that I only learned about it through the jagged filter of my mother, who always spun it with sarcastic remarks like "He was brought up by a nice enough Irish Catholic family but was never smart enough to accept their help or advice, only their love of beer."

It is true. One of his favorite things to say was "Beer is my best friend." I think mine is wine.

But he had enough fight in him to make a life for himself. With a tenth-grade education, he worked his way up in banking from emptying garbage pails to functioning in middle management, assistant vice president, which, whatever that meant, got him a desk and a chair but never an office.

In the early '80s, when an MBA became the GED of the finance industry, he was passed over time and again, and they eventually sent him back to the streets to pursue customers who were behind on their mortgage payments. "Chasing slows," he used to call it. "I'm on the outside looking in," he'd grumble as he reached for his black overcoat on the rack by the front door.

They'd handed a life-altering humiliation to a man who'd prided himself on his talent for choosing good accounts. At his funeral, a couple who'd gotten their mortgage approved by him many years before came to me and said, "Your father saved us. When the bank didn't want to give us our loan, he personally came to our apartment, dined with us, listened to us, met our children, and then went back and told the bank that he had faith in our future. We'll never forget him for that."

The meek inheriting the earth.

Now it's all computers and credit scores. When that was starting, they pushed my father into his red Pontiac Bonneville, tossed him a wind-up Polaroid instant camera, and assigned him to sit outside these "slows'" homes and photograph their properties and belongings for potential repossession—and, if possible, document any behavior that might show financial shenanigans.

"On the outside looking in"—through the lens of a Polaroid camera, and the bottom of a beer glass. This was the refrain of his heaviest drinking days, high school for me. "In the rain, in the snow," he'd grumble to himself, his lower jaw clenched like a fist as he threw the contents of his pockets into his desk drawer after coming home from work and a few hours at Chick's Bar.

Dad remained an almost silent man at home, except for those Saturday Evening Soliloquies, the overture of which opened with the crashes and thuds of dishes and chairs being banged around in the kitchen. Then he'd get angry about the dishes. "Three sets of dishes," one dirty on the counter, one soaking dirty in the sink, and one clean in the rack, not yet put away. "Pile up . . . Pile up . . . Pile up," he'd say, pushing his arm into the garbage can to compress it down. And he'd sweep—sweep and sweep—at the floor furiously, poking and jabbing the broom down in quick strokes. "I can do this. See me? My sons can't do this? Look at me. I can do it." I have three older brothers. And eventually, "My sons—they're NOTHING," he'd spew, and then he'd trod down a repetitive, ugly, curse-laden list of filial disappointments, calling all of us out. (Ally, being the oldest, was out of the house by then, lucky her.) But I wasn't "nothing" then. I'd been president of my high school class, Latin Club president, playing trombone professionally in a wedding band and a local-events concert band.

What he said to his pals at Chick's all those hours after work each day, I'll never know. They weren't helping him, that I do know. Likely, they spent their words bitching about their own problems in a deeply depressed decade of an already dead town, saved by the fact that bar glasses of Stegmaier beer were only thirty-five cents each. Wilkes-Barre, Pennsylvania. I couldn't wait to get myself out. I would never get trapped there. And I was going to be something big, not a cog. But I've failed at everything, and I'm "on the outside looking in." And I've turned to alcohol, because it's good—and it's my friend. And I'm frustrated and disappointed and angry and sad, like my father, and they're good. In the moment, these things disguise themselves as useful. They pass the wretched time.

And now, from having gone next door, I know that Irene's life is a mess that I couldn't have imagined. And I feel I'm no better off than my father.

4:00 AM

Still up, can't get my heart rate down. The Roxy box keeps calling out to me. I need to get rid of it, but I also want to go in and touch her things one last time. Her perfume is still on her clothes like flowers that won't perish. It's in the cardboard now. OK, I admit, I just did that. Her fragrance is like wine. I've also had some wine, and by some, I mean I don't know how much. My mother used to count my dad's beers. She's not around to count mine. I also had some pot-infused goldfish that my friend Nick gave me a while ago. I'm so tired. And wired.

My mother used to say, "No matter how bad you feel, there's always someone else in the world who has it worse." Well, everyone else in the world who has it worse can take it easy for a day, because it's finally spun around to me. I think I'd be better off just gone. Gone . . . gone. I've thought about doing it. I love how Fredric March walks into the ocean at the end of *A Star Is Born*. But I'm a good swimmer. I'd have to weigh myself down with some kind of anchor, a ball and chain or something, and drag it along the sand as I plod into the tide. Not nearly as elegant as the movie. Maybe I can just suffocate myself under a stack of overdue bills. Calculate myself to death. Second-guess myself to death. I could double up on this dog log with a hunger strike. But that's no good without publicity. Is there anything sadder than an unpublicized hunger strike? "He starved himself, apparently, while writing in this log here." Coroner's diagnosis: he thought himself to death.

You either give up or fight, I guess.

December 27, 7:00 AM

What a night. Didn't sleep. My apartment is freezing. There's no insulation in these old places. At least I have space heaters. Irene's is probably worse. Lauren started barking at 6:30. She probably didn't sleep either. I'm sure Irene'll be home soon. Hospitals always rush you out for release first thing in the morning.

11:45 AM

Cloudy, chilly day. I haven't heard any human activity at Irene's. If she's not coming home today, then surely someone will come over to get the dogs. I can't face stepping into that sulfur mine again. I don't care if they piss and shit. If Irene didn't care, why should I?

Every creative bone in my body has been gnawed to dust. I have to design a logo and website for an anesthesia consultants group in Culver City. They're having a meeting some time after New Year's, so they want to see something, but I can't fucking think. I haven't even done the logo looks, let alone the site.

I wonder if I could bargain with them for some anesthesia. How nice it would be to slip away right now—loopy with sedation. A pretty nurse talking to me in calming tones, touching her hips to my cheek for a moment as she leans over to reach for that wonderful rubberized mask that she's going to set so gently over my nose and mouth.

"Breathe in, Richard. Relax and breathe normally. You look very handsome today. Do you mind if I caress your cheek whilst you go to sleep?"

She might say "whilst." She's an Elizabethan princess, too.

Help me, Nurse Princess—help me escape Sophie sensory over-load.

"Don't you mean Lauren, my sweet?" she'd ask.

"Yes, my angel, Lauren too. Save me from them all."

I could die this way.

In high school, my friend Paul's mother was a nurse at Mercy Hospital—and among my most prized female fantasies. One night an ambulance took me to their ER after a car accident. A pal and I had been out partying. I was in the passenger seat of his Ford Pinto wagon, no seat belt. Not his fault. Both of us had been acting nuts that night, blowing off steam. The car swerved and hit a lamppost. My face went through the windshield and back. Paul's mother held my hand while I got hundreds of stitches on the left side of my face, forehead, and neck—whilst I got them. They wouldn't knock me out because of the head wounds. I had to watch the needle coming at me, ripping at me, over and over, and she whispered in my ear to keep me calm and strong. If I can make it through that, I can make it through this. I still have scars on my jaw, face, and forehead. You'll see them. I cherish that painful moment with her.

12:20 PM

I guess if no one shows up by 2:00 or 3:00, I'll go over and throw some food in their bowls again. Lauren's barking, but at least there's reason in it in that dark, forgotten well. No less irritating though.

Irene only broke her arm or something. She was awake and talking and everything when they took her in the ambulance. You'd think she'd call a friend or someone about her dogs. Then again, why should she start to have true consideration for her dogs at this point? I'm not surprised, are you?

1:00 PM

How long can dogs go without eating? Pretty long, right? Aren't there stories of dogs walking for weeks to find their masters—going across state lines—over deserts and mountains? I guess they find some way to eat though. Would these two Yorkies? We can go for weeks. I'm sure dogs are tougher than we are because they don't think into the future, and stress, and get killed by the sadness, right?

I guess water is the issue. We can only go without it for a few days, I think. That's why those survival guys on TV are always pissing into evacuated snake skins and carrying them around their necks. Well, those two dogs have plenty of piss puddles in the kitchen to keep them alive.

If something happens to the dogs, here I am writing about my knowing that they're there unattended. So, is this somehow my responsibility now? How ridiculous is that? What right has she to abandon her animals like this and then blame me if they dry out to death? A pet owner is supposed to have a plan in case of emergency, aren't they? And does a broken arm keep her from calling a friend or telling a nurse about her stupid dogs? I'm certainly not going to take care of them.

You've smelled death, right, Sheriff? They take you to the morgue like in the old TV opening of *Quincy, M.E.* when they show the rookie cops fainting at an autopsy, right? Well, over there it's living death, an abscessed malodor that reproduces upon itself as the bacteria chews it down and then the dogs replenish it from the top. If things were normal, maybe, but it's a horrid nightmare, and I shouldn't have to go face it just because I happen to be living the closest. Nope. I absolve myself of responsibility. I don't even have to do that. I have no responsibility to absolve myself of. What I am doing is refusing to take responsibility here. It's an entirely proper reverse "moral imperative." I didn't create that hell over there, and I didn't raise two untrained, hurly-burly-haired monsters in my home.

2:25 PM

Holy God, I was just over there. So much worse in the daylight. Have you ever been inside a hoarder's house, Sheriff? This is not like one of those cases on TV where you have to climb over things to get from place to place, but it is the hoarding of someone who is seriously messed up.

I covered my nose and mouth again with my T-shirt and tossed some food and water into the bowls. What a stench. The dogs are nasty. I don't mean that in a biting way. I don't think they'd bite me because they're responding to me a little more calmly already. Although, if one of them did bite me, I'd probably go down in five seconds, considering the bacteria that they're able to house in their jaws and gums with built-up resistance. I'm not touching them because they're so dirty, and these aren't "visits." This is just feeding.

I'm hoping by the end of the afternoon someone'll come by.

6:30 PM

Are dogs supposed to be fed once or twice a day? I've never had a dog, and it's not something you think about until two of them are staring up at you. I can't let them starve over there, even if Irene can. If she's not home by 8:00 tonight, I'll go and feed them again.

7:30 PM

"It's the First Law of Karma," Ally says to me.

"These are laws to you people?"

"They're called laws because they govern human nature, inescapably."

"Inexplicably?"

"You know, you're the one who keeps asking about karma. It's simple, the Law of Attraction: like attracts like. So who you are is what you will bring into your life."

"Well, I have nobody in my life. So that means I'm nobody."

"You're an incredible pessimist."

"You cannot defeat a defeatist, Ally. We always win."

"By losing."

"By knowing. Come over to our side. The expectations are so much easier."

"Pessimism is low tone and could lead to death."

"That's optimistic. OK then—I'm completely alone, sad, angry, poor, frustrated, powerless, and depressed, not to mention out of shape. The person that I had 'attracted' is gone."

"You have to deal with that."

"I want to 'attract' her back."

"You know I think you should move on. I hate seeing you hurt."

"But I can figure this out. She saw me as resisting, or hesitating, or something. Maybe, deep down, for some reason, I was—Mom and Dad, something, the house we grew up in."

"But when you love somebody, you don't leave them. You believe in them, even when they no longer believe in themselves."

"She made me happy."

"That's another thing, Richard. You have a 'You-Make-Me' complex: 'Roxy makes me so happy' or 'Irene makes me so mad.' Do you realize how much control you give other people over your own life?"

Sheriff, people don't make you happy, angry, sad? You arrest a perp, he spits at you and kicks you in the balls, you don't get angry? And that stuff doesn't pile up on you and make you an angry person? Conversely, doesn't your wife—even just seeing her—make you happy? Your kids, with that wonderful, unadulterated innocence?

"I was in love, Ally. Please."

"Your happiness has to come from within, not from someone else."

"It's not possible. Look, since I've un-attracted Roxy, what do I have as the prominent forces in my life? A barking dog and a bitter old woman."

"The Third Law of Karma: whatever you resist persists in you."

"Another law?"

"Whatever you pay the most attention to is what you're going to experience. Doesn't that make sense to you?"

"Sorry, I wasn't paying attention."

"You're actually not. Who's the one who's always complaining about everything—me or you? When you were at school, did you teach the kids to empower themselves, or did you tell them not to bother because circumstance would always control them anyhow?"

"Maybe Irene attracted me. It's her fault then. But if 'like attracts like,' then that means that I'm 'like' her, and I'm a wretched human being."

"Well, you're certainly seeming wretched."

"I should have moved in with Roxy—"

"With her roommate? You're both too old for that. Richard, she is not the answer to everything, not anymore. She made that choice."

"I should have figured something out."

"How's your shingles?"

"I should be a roofer. Actually, it's clearing up, finally."

"That olive leaf extract is amazing. It helps with blood pressure, too. It's also supposed to help with cognitive decline, though I see no evidence that it's helping you with that yet. Seriously, you have to deal with your stress. One step you could take would be to let Roxy go and move on."

"I can't."

Ally's too angry at Roxy to discuss me having any hope. She doesn't buy that couples can get back together successfully after a breakup. You don't know any who have? They can. End of conversation.

I'm not supposed to be thinking about Roxy somehow? I can't change my feelings. I can't move anything. In fact, the Greek philosopher Zeno pointed out that in order to get from one place to another, one first would have to get halfway there, but before getting to that initial halfway point, you'd have to get halfway to an earlier halfway point—and so on—in constantly divisible halfway points through minuscule infinitely. Since we can never get halfway to any halfway point because there's always a newer halfway point, then we can never move to any new space. That is my heart.

8:30 PM

Just fed them. It's like trying to catch a roach with greased chopsticks. I'm keeping their bowls separate so that I know they've both eaten. But by the time I'd gotten food into one bowl, they were both at it, pushing each other, and when I got food in the second bowl, they both rushed to get to that bowl. Then one would decide to rush back, and this would start a whole series of the two of them chasing after the food bowls and pushing each other out of the way as if battling for a salt lick rolling in the dirt at a Soviet gulag. They are expending so many calories with this feeding system that it's burning off its own usefulness. I don't know whose bowl is whose, and, for that matter, there were two different types of dry dog food, and I didn't know which food was for which, so I might have been the cause of the frenzy. But still, they were totally undignified. I yelled at them to settle down, but after taking one deep breath with which to shout, I had to get outside for fresh air.

That's it for tonight. I've done my duty. They can shit and piss all they like in their feral zoo. I don't want to touch them. As barbarian as they are when they're eating, they might be even more wild with me if I try walking them. I'm sure Irene will be back tomorrow or the next day, and everything'll be back to abnormal.

December 28, 10:15 AM

Put some food in their bowls, fresh water. So gross I can't take it. It's hell inside Irene's.

Speaking of hell—Will correctly predicted that "Johnny Cash moment" in the jail, Sheriff. I did write a song about that Richard Ramirez visit. It's called "Lawyers and Mothers." It's on my album. The style of it, we think—or hoped—was kind of like if Eddie Vedder mixed with Bono and Neil Young and made a solo album. Man, I played every club in town back then, got so close to record deals with A&M, Geffen, and Virgin, despite my lousy managers. It felt great—for Roxy, too—who energized me every note of the way. The retail chain Tower Records picked up my record. I even did an in-store acoustic concert at their famed Sunset Boulevard location. They wheeled the racks of CDs around to make room for a stage and an audience. Put up huge photos and posters of the album, my name on the marquee outside. I played guitar and sang. My producer, who was the accordion player with Oingo Boingo, played. My friend Scott played tenor sax, and I had a percussionist. So many friends took the day off to be there. Roxy took two personal days because she knew we'd be celebrating late into the night.

Turned out to be my last gig ever, however, though I didn't know that at the time. That Tower Records store sat right across the street from Geffen. So many times, they'd promised to come see me play—but this gig meant for sure. During every song, as I played and sang, all I did was look past my friends and fans, trying to see if the dude from Geffen had shown up. That's not where I wanted my head to be. Geffen didn't show—again.

Tower Records is gone now. Their dream ended, too. That spot is now a clothing store.

When I first got to L.A., I happened to meet Ray Manzarek, keyboard player from the Doors, at an Armstrong Home Improvement store. I stood behind him in the checkout line trying to figure out how to start a conversation, while he paid for three hanging plants. He was very friendly. In the parking lot he told me, "You can't wake up every day, Richard, and say, 'I hope I become a rock star today.' You have to say, 'I'm going to write a great song today.' That's what Jim and I did." And that's what I tried to do, Sheriff. That's what I tried.

I walked away from teaching after seven years, inspired to pursue my music career. I'd been teaching kids to pursue their dreams, but I hadn't fully committed to my own yet. Now I'm a "former musician"—only in L.A. can you become a "former musician." If you don't make it big, there's no way to make decent money.

I'm a "former teacher," too. Former dreamer. Former boyfriend. Former sane person. Current nothing. Certainly, choosing fonts and moving triangles around a backlit screen for people as a graphic designer isn't what I'd pictured for my life.

What can I do for money now? I was a damn good teacher. But I'm not going back. Bottom line: the kids are great, the adults suck. Year after year they hand you a new, stifling curriculum, the result of weeklong conferences in Palm Springs or Santa Barbara, each just another political ploy to keep downtown and state administrators' positions rationalized and well paid with no thought of teacher innovation.

Besides that, a lot of the teachers were awful—lazy, often not educated in the fields they were teaching, entirely untrained for the classroom atmosphere, too many with their own personal or political agendas, with no sense of how to teach, or inspire, or empower via the subject matter at hand.

A school system that can't even keep the restrooms maintained—or safe—is not somewhere one wants to invest one's life unless it's a divine vocation. Yes, I left for music, but I also considered myself a conscientious objector.

On top of it, my teaching assistant that year, Luis, was murdered outside of his apartment building. Gang members followed him home from an ATM and shot him seven times in the chest when he got out of his car. His mother was visiting from Panama, her first time in the United States. She heard the gunfire. His funeral totaled me. I'd had a student die in each year that I taught. Then Luis. Life is very brief. It isn't the length of the candle, it's the fight of the flame against the whims of the breeze.

Roxy totally supported my decision to leave teaching at the time. Even she is working on her doctorate because she wants to move up to higher education and out of the K–12 system.

Was I right to leave that path, Sheriff? Do you think that our teachers are any better now than when you were young? Are the children safer? Are they better served now with regard to the basic knowledge necessary to strive and succeed? Are your kids in public school or private?

So . . . anyway, one of the songs is about the prison visit. You can hear it if or when we meet.

3:00 PM

Just got an e-mail from Roxy. Seeing her name in my inbox was like stepping out of the shower and being tasered. I have such fear of her saying that she doesn't want to work things out or, worse, of her being condescending with friendliness. God. I don't want to be pitied by anyone but myself.

Wasn't good—a bunch of hairsplitting fuss about a New Year's party we'd both been invited to, about how maybe we should attend at separate times so that no one's uncomfortable. Who gets midnight? She does—because I wasn't going to go anyway. No one would miss a sorry sack like me right now.

The mutual friends mesh is brutal. I've been on a long break from everyone. Space. Isolation. Except you. Even still, I've had a couple uncomfortable instances where people have obviously been groping their way through heavily redacted information so as not to hurt me, or give me hope, or trigger whatever any word about Roxy would do. I've been off social media. If there's going to be any communication, it's going to be direct.

Not going to a dumb party shows how broken I am. But I don't want a new year. And I can't handle seeing her face, her eyes—like a drowning man's last glimpse upward at the rippling sky.

I didn't respond. Stasya told me not to. "Don't be small," she said. All I want to discuss is how we can try to work things out, the value of our seven years together, not the minutiae of our new social comings and goings. I'm cutting off all goings anyhow. Does she miss me? She did contact me, right?

December 29, 11:20 AM

Played it smart today. Before I went to Irene's, I put on a painter's mask and latex gloves that I had from when Roxy and I did my kitchen. I also put plastic grocery bags from Ralphs over my sneakers so I don't have to clean my shoes after every visit anymore. The mask convinces me that the smell isn't forming directly into a mass of cells that will encrust in my nasal passages, only to await the best moment to snap apart and shoot into my brain. I'm making a path for myself through the living room into the kitchen so that I can walk without having to step over crap or knock over piles. I also cleaned a small square of the kitchen floor near the sink where I can stand to wash their bowls and get their food and water together without feeling the living sludge slithering beneath my shoes.

I'm using Formula 409 "antibacterial" all-purpose cleaner. It brags about killing "99.9% of viruses & bacteria." I can attest that the remaining 0.1% has a mighty life to it.

With every swirl of the paper towels, vibrations of stench scrape across my face as the linoleum is unearthed. It's actually eggshell white under there. Of all the people who cannot handle a white kitchen floor. I feel like a cosmetic dentist that's been airdropped into Appalachia. The dogs run around madly as I get them something to eat from the dog food bags on the counter. I'm careful not to knock over anything piled up there—pots and pans, bags, Tupperware. There's a defeated stick of butter, fused to its wrapper. The garbage is on the counter, too. I imagine that's to keep it away from the dogs, though having it sit at the level of the human nose doesn't make it pleasing. I accidentally drop pellets of food as I move things around, and the dogs scurry to scarf them up like fish in a bowl. I've heard that dogs' mouths have a better ability to protect against infection, but I'm positive that they haven't yet evolved enough to combat this kind of pathogen stew. Irene will be home at any moment, I'm sure. Until then, they'll survive.

8:00 PM

Roxy. Love is brutal. Fuck. And without it, it's all I think about. Love is a servant of abuse. I understand why people shoot heroin. Loneliness. Your heart has disappeared, so you have to manufacture one. My father's opium den, Chick's Bar, was three blocks from our house up North Main Street, across from St. John's church and Merritt Hughes Funeral Home. He was a lonely man. The last time he and my mom had sex was on the night of Ally's high school graduation. "Cut off," he always said, with blunt force trauma. "Cut off." And that's that for the rest of one's life? Catholic or not, he had five kids, and, though he showed us more disdain than affection, he wasn't going to leave his family. Amazing.

Is Roxy right? Am I unable to love anything? I mean, commitment is love, yes, but . . .

I never got a "love" talk. In college when I told my parents that my then girlfriend and I were in love, Dad said, "What is this love shit?" Before that, any kind of sex talk was out of the question from someone who'd been "cut off." Plus, I went to Catholic high school, so, supposedly, sex itself was out of the question, and we all should have been cut off. To supplant that forced ignorance, my friends Mack, Reggie, Paul, and I used to go to a XXX drive-in theater, the Oak Hill, up in Moosic Township, just south of Scranton. It was right off the exit from Interstate 81. You could see the films going through the vertical slits between the trees as your car sped by down the highway. We called it the Stroke Hill, naturally. They showed the just-one-step-beyond-softcore movies: Jenna Jameson, Savannah, Nici Sterling—these women blew our minds. We weren't there for a circle jerk. We went there to see sex, to look at it, learn what it was, how women worked, where body parts were. . . . No, we didn't discuss it like a science lab. We joked about it with false bravado. We'd sneak in a case of Miller eight-ounce ponies, get drunk, and laugh and make fun of everything—on the outside. But individually, deep down, we were fighting against repression. Each of us anticipated future sex like a tsunami warning, and needed to be ready to keep it from becoming a catastrophe. Controversial in the community as it was, and we were certainly blinding ourselves to the dark side of porn at the time, we let the Stroke Hill do us a tremendous service by being there in the pitiful absence of any other options.

The closest I got to a sex talk from Dad was five words: "Keep it in your pants." He'd caught me masturbating one night against the freezer door in the utility room. I guess I'd made a sound and woken him up off the couch. Earlier that evening, Dawn Lombardeli had been dry-rubbing my crotch like she was kneading dough at her father's pizza shop, and I couldn't hold it in.

"Keep it in your pants," was all he said, and he walked away. Hard to argue the clarity and logic of that advice, birth-control-wise, but as for ever actually pleasing a woman, loving her, understanding her needs and desires, it fell woefully short, like the nights at the Stroke Hill did.

I finished and cleaned up with Windex as was my dignified teen protocol. The freezer itself, which stored various meats of London broil, hamburger, and kielbasa—sexy as that was—didn't particularly make me horny. The sheet steel door just seemed easy to wipe up, I'd thought, and there was no other privacy in the house. Now I'd ruined that, too, because on that night I couldn't "keep it in my pants."

My dad had that very distinct car in those years, that red Bonneville. One night when my buddies and I were in seminar at the Stroke Hill, I was taking a moment to look around, giving my brain a respite from the hundred-foot screen of genital wrestling, and suddenly I saw, six rows over, that very something so distinct and familiar, and before I could register the permanent impact that words can have, I reflexively announced, "Hey, there's my dad." He was slouched in the driver's seat of his car, tired eyes staring forward, the metal speaker hung on the door, the same cool blue from the screen falling on his face as was on ours.

The screaming silence of awkward acknowledgment filled the van like sarin gas. Mack broke the hush. "Here's to the Old Man," he said, raising his Miller pony for a toast. "He knows how to have a good time." We all laughed, mine forced. "To the Old Man," we said, and we clinked our small bottles together and chugged the beers.

Mack must have sensed this to be a good time to leave. He started the engine and the van crept out. No one spoke as the tires crunched over the gravel of the unpaved lot. None of us wanted to be spotted there, though how could my father narc on us in this circumstance?

Looking back, as embarrassed as I was, I think my friends understood. I doubt any of their parents, all still Catholic-together then, were having sex anymore. We'd all been given a lesson on marriage and how drearily long life can be. And my dad still had sixteen years to live after that.

These were my early examples of the joys of love and sex, and the benefits of long-term commitment. Oh, my private trombone teacher showed me his penis once when I was thirteen. God bless him, he was actually a really good guy. He took care of me as somewhat of a surrogate father. We went fishing. He taught me how to work on cars, made me a really good musician. I earned an offer of a music scholarship from Carnegie Mellon because of him. Mr. White cared for me. But that day, after a lesson at his house, he'd asked if I'd ever seen an uncircumcised penis, which I hadn't, and before I could say, "What?" I was seeing one. I didn't like it. He wanted me to touch it "to see how the extra flesh worked." I just said no, and that was that—really. He put it and its mysterious skin sheath away. Neither of us ever mentioned it again. I've never told anybody because he was such a beloved person, and at least he'd respected my response. It didn't register to me as a sex offense at the time. I'd heard rumors of much worse floating around about the priests anyhow. Love and sex. I think he loved me. His commitment to my happiness never wavered. I studied with him from age nine to seventeen. And I loved him. I did, just not like that.

I'm starting to feel like that psych ward prisoner at the county jail. I have terrible nights on that cot of my own—thinking of Roxy, thinking and thinking—unable to change things, unable to feel good, unable to stop thinking, wishing for a prayer. I want to disappear. If I had a gun, I really think I could put it to my head and squeeze the fuck out of the trigger. It's been over three and a half months, and I still live with my need for Roxy like a sixth sense. I've found a porn star online that reminds me of her—Aria. Geez, I know her name: blue eyes—same long black hair—legs all the way to her neck. Almost similar face somehow, or I make it that way. I look for scenes of her alone. It's backbreaking. A borderline sickness, this demanding substitution. Or a survival mechanism. A preservation through destructive behavior. I know how bad porn is. I know how cheap and filthy and dangerous and awful and exploitive it is. But I watch them in silence. It's horrible. I torture myself. But I need to see her moving, talking, even in facsimile, because it sparks specific memories, and I project those memories onto the moving facade, and that orgasm, even tangential through imagination, still feels like no other—when my mind locks onto it, it feels like life. But immediately after, it's a washout; fifteen seconds is not enough rain of mercy to heal a desert. I shouldn't. I'd get rid of the Internet if my work didn't depend on it. It's there all the time, and the ventral striatum of my brain is itching for its reward stimulation. Ironically, it was Roxy who taught me the most about the biology of behavior while immersed in her grad school work. That was sexier than any lipstick or knee-high boots.

The Internet is an addictive outlet that sadistically offers a match light in the pit of despair. But it's even less real than fantasy. I've got to block myself somehow.

11:15 PM

God, I love Stasya. She told me no note in the box but to get it sent. "You are the strong one. Be strong, Richard. You don't need words. She knows what is in your heart."

She does know. No note. Sent the box.

December 30, 10:00 AM

Hit with a jolt this morning. My neighbor Jazmine had told me a few days ago that there'd be a moving truck in the driveway today. She's found a guest house in Hancock Park, "It's safer there." But I'd forgotten. I'm happy for her, but the thought of a moving truck being here—it's jarring. Time is passing. Change is happening. I've suddenly been here for ten years.

I was woken up by the spinning squeaks of the dolly wheels as they passed by my window under the tremendous weight of Jazmine's packed-up sequins. The movers are still here. They shout commands to one another in Spanish, Jazmine too. They sound so happy and enthusiastic. I can't take it. The commotion is making Lauren freak out. I'm surrounded like Custer. Come on, Cheyenne. Come on, Arapaho. Stop all the mad shenanigans—just close the circle, and take me out already.

God, I hope my rent check clears.

Work is so slow. No chance for unemployment, because I've been self-employed. What a fucked-up system. Fucked-up credit.

And my car's too old to even sign up for a rideshare thing, plus any of those gigs jack your car insurance through the roof.

This motionlessness of mine must end, one way or another. Dogs' lives are motionless. But it's OK; they don't think about the future. I envy that.

It's forty feet from my door to Irene's. Am I one wall away from the very picture of my own lonely future? How much of this is fate? Is suicide fate? On calls, Sheriff, every person you encounter is in a moment of whirling distress. How much of that is fate versus choices? You arrest people because of their actions—their choices—not their fate, right? It's part of my fate that I am here, broke and alone. Irene is in the hospital, broke—broken—and alone. The mutts next door are dog-broke, not housebroken, and alone. How much of the world is the same?

If what I'm feeling is my own self being destroyed, then how far does this have to go before it's just done with? It's over with Roxy. I'm just fucking stupid with everything. *Over* can be such an inviting word. You can't run the distance, and nothingness will finally do—so *over* it is.

My friend Stuart, a piano player, had written a wonderful musical called *Family* about a divorced man who wants to bring his family back together, full of lift and hope. The songs were big and melodic, made for Broadway. It never sold. Stuart eventually drank himself to death, vodka. It took him ten hard years to fight off life.

The comedian Richard Jeni, a very successful man, several HBO specials, etc., shot himself in the head, forty-nine years old, in his condo just about five blocks from here. You may have even been in on that call, were you? Kurt Cobain is dead. Heath Ledger. Whitney Houston. Spalding Gray. Hunter S. Thompson. Soldiers—strong men and women—come back from the Middle East tormented, and it steals their will to live. The mind is everything devastating.

Mark Twain, in his late twenties, wrote to his brother, "If I do not get out of debt in three months—pistols or poison for one—exit me."

Exit me.

But how? Hamlet stages a scene where the king is killed quickly and peacefully by having poison poured into his ear as he slept. It's a most merciful of murders. That's how I'd want it. Doesn't involve swallowing, pulling a trigger, no cutting—just drops. The poison is called hebenon. It isn't real. Fuck. They think it was supposed to be hemlock, which is what Socrates used to kill himself in submitting to the Athenian execution order. But Plato called it pharmakon, which also doesn't exist. So there, hemlock is just a sweet illusion.

Socrates's death crept along in a slow-moving paralysis that began in his feet and legs and worked up to his heart and mind. Plato writes that Socrates expressed no stress, because he didn't fear death. Perhaps it's something not to be feared, especially if it has a purpose. Can there be inspirational suicides? Well, it is in my blood—Dad's mom, remember? Perhaps it shouldn't be feared. Thanks, Grandma.

Napoleon swallowed poison while in exile at Elba, but it didn't work. What hell that must be. Dying in one's sleep is the dream, and here I am—can't even sleep. It's so punishing, dysfunctioning. The battleships go out of line, and the fight turns to spinning chaos on the battering waves. How do men sleep in prison? Can exhaustion finally carry the wretched to rest?

I'm beaten. But I am still functioning—at least enough to check in on the dogs again and clean another few square inches. I still get some work done. Regardless of sleep, I drag myself to the front room and engage the computer and try to fulfill client requests.

Self-pity. I don't care, it feels good. It's satisfying. Fuck you. That's the trouble with all this writing what's in my head and heart. It's too much reflection. Too much time in the mirror—threads of indulgence weave upon themselves until it becomes the only way you think.

December 31, 10:35 AM

I apologize for the rambling last night. Those dogs are getting to me. And the end of a year. I'm in a bad place right now. I have so much to sort out. It's late morning already. Have to go over there and feed them.

10:55 AM

Man, they are not house-trained at all. Behind the door is a minefield of wet dog mush, barely discernible against the sullied, browned carpet but for the morning light that glances off its newer moisture. I tiptoe to avoid what's fresh from what's permanent. The rug, bounteously threadbare, looks to have been some sort of fancy Asian carpet—ornate blue base with exotic florals woven in pink and white with vines (I think those were the colors). It's like a tapestry. Was. Now it's a crapestry, a huge biomass obstruction like so much used Charmin.

And I know there will be a second new mess in the kitchen or bedroom, too, waiting for me as their expected guest. Those dogs have no shame. They go in different places. And who knows which is doing what where, and when?

The plastic Ralphs bags wrapping my shoes weep their soft crackle as I carefully navigate the muddy Straits of Dog Doo. My feet sweat. My hands sweat in the gloves, and my nose sweats from the hot fog of my own carbon dioxide trapped within the mask.

The dogs dart from room to room. They separate and run around, hair flipping wildly, then find one another again to bump noses. Then they run in opposite directions again. They must be frightened of me, especially considering this semisurgical/alien-just-landed outfit. Most of my face is covered—and will remain that way—so my voice comes to them from nowhere.

I clean their dishes and give them fresh food and water. Nelson's tongue beats at the water as if it owes him money. The long hair around his face falls into the bowl and then gets lapped up into his mouth. They can't keep it out of their mouths when they eat, and then it stays there, soaked, caked, and nested for the day.

In the living room, a color catches my eye. High up, there's a collection of blue-and-white drawn-on-style vases collecting dust on top of a bookcase. They look like something Chinese, something someone would collect. I notice a Chinese theme. There's a series of small mirrors with Chinese figures painted on them above the bookcases near the ceiling, too high for me to get to. So hard to imagine that she once decorated, like an entirely different person. But the air is squeezing me out.

I hadn't mentioned the bookcases, Sheriff, had I? They go around three walls in the front room, from the floor to the ceiling. It's an impressive library collection crammed into a tiny space, mostly hardcover classics, though now tainted and untouchable. Books about dogs. Damn Yorkies. Lots of classic literature. Some art books. Two walls of books, actually. One of the walls of shelves is filled mostly with videocassettes. Easily over a thousand of them—the canon of film, all the greats, some amazing film noir. I wonder if the tumor affected her ability to read? What a difference if so, books to videotape.

January

January 1, 11:30 AM

Ally had suggested to me that I write down my dreams. I haven't been doing it because they're all bad, and, by the way, I'm already doing a log about the stuff when I'm awake. But last night the new year rumbled in with some real choice nocturnal pain: Roxy and I got married. The full wedding shebang: the rehearsal dinner, everyone there—friends, old and new, family—the ceremony itself, my brother as best man, a brunch celebration the next morning, nicely detailed even with the appropriate hangovers.

She never stopped smiling, shining with joy and grace. Exchanging those vows with her induced the most "right" feeling I'd ever experienced. When I woke up, I was happy, calm, secure, confident, proud—everything good that I don't get to really feel. It drops me into the body of a brazen bull, the ancient Greek bronze torture device, to be cooked alive by the tyranny of my own disappointment. Last night, the first New Year's Eve in a long time passed without a midnight kiss for love and luck.

I finally have a night without a bad dream, and this good dream makes it worse. If I can't control my mind any longer—if it's not

the heartache, it's the finances, the dream death, the barking. The
failure of controlling my own cerebral cineplex—pictures and scenes
so vivid. I want it to stop, everything.

5:15 PM

Dinnertime. The dogs don't have collars on. They have no tags or
licenses, or anything hanging around their necks. Aren't they supposed to be registered, like guns, or a sex offender? What if one of
them got out? This amazes me. If I had a dog, I'd be in constant
fear of that. Everyone talks so much about dogs and loyalty. All they
want to do is get out the door and run away. When I was young,
I saw my oldest brother's dog, Pete, get hit by a car. My brother'd
rescued the sad, black, rib-showing, gangly street urchin from an
alleyway behind a bar after he'd seen someone pour a pitcher of beer
over the poor thing's head. I saw Pete run right out the screen door,
down the stairs and into the street, no comprehension of danger.
Then SLAM, and Pete was dying. I'll never understand dog owners
who walk their dogs with no leash. This is a busy town. Makes no
sense to me.

It's been several days since Irene fell. I've decided to try to take
the dogs outside for some real air. The only leashes I'd found in the
apartment were these thin rope things with a noose at the end that
tightens with a plastic slider. They're like piano wire. If the dogs pull
at all—which they will—they'll slice themselves into pieces. So, I
went over to Tailwaggers on Fairfax and bought two regular leashes
and two harness-type collars. Modern gender identity debates aside,
I got a pink set for Lauren and royal blue for Nelson. They wrap
around and underneath each of their front legs and then up over
their shoulders and backs. I'd strap them in like fighter pilots.

When I got into Irene's apartment, I used my teacher authority
voice to tell them that they were going outside and that they were
going to behave.

"One leg at a time into the harness, Nelson—one, right, then
two, left. You'll get used to the system."

There were several, *"Come here"*s, a few *"Stop it"*s, some *"Nelson!"*s, a couple *"Don't be a baby, Lauren!"*s, but we got through it. Harnesses on and leashes hooked, I patted each one on the head, and we were ready to go. It surprised me how they responded to my touch with calm. Maybe they like latex? Their eyes squinted at me a little bit, as if I were shining a flashlight at them.

As we walked to the door, my heart raced. *Once I get them outside, if something happens to one of them, it's my fault.*

When I open the door, they both suddenly dart straight out to the two stairs. Lauren's leash slips from my hand and I kneel down and grab it. I am now intimately involved in Irene's living room rug sludge, right at one of their favorite spots to go by the door. Before I can say, "Oh . . . FUCK," squeals belt through the air outside. Lauren is dangling off of the first step, the one that'd tripped up Sophie before her. To them, it's like a three-story building.

"Hey, you dum-dums!" I yelled as I got up. "Those are steps! You have to wait for me. I'm in charge here, not you."

The two faces of fear looked up at me—Nelson, afraid of my anger, and Lauren, having just cleared a near-death experience, the fear of the "undiscover'd country." My face was probably not much different. *This is a big mistake. One or both of these dogs is going to die out here.* The rubber of the gloves helps me grip the leashes tightly as I wrap them around my wrists, and I tell myself that we have to go forward. If I turn back now, then these dum-dums win. They're pulling full force at the leashes. They want to go for a walk, or they want to get away from me. I'm sweating, and my shirt's damp with the seasoned slime that'd splashed up from the rug. The painter's mask hangs below my chin, and its rubber band pinches the fuzz on the back of my neck like a family of wasps.

Why am I here? Why am I doing this? Why are they so wild? How does Irene do this?

I hold them still as I turn to lock the door behind us. The last thing I need is someone walking in and snooping around while we're gone. Of course, God bless anyone who wants to burgle that residence. The only thing to steal would be a pulmonary infection.

Still, I look at those blue and white vases and think maybe they have some value to her. They're not going to be stolen while I'm in charge.

Screw it. You know what, Sheriff? I didn't lock the door. I didn't because I walked back inside. I panicked. I thought, *If one of the dogs got away, I'd be totally screwed—for trying to help.* They pulled against me as I yanked them back in. I've been cleaning up their messes every day anyhow. I might as well get used to it until Irene gets back.

This was just walking dogs for God's sake. But these two aren't predictable—and it's two against one.

I don't know why I wanted to do it in the first place.

I need to get outside, too, Sheriff, but I have nowhere to go. Being around people is punishing. I don't understand their happiness.

You know, this dog garbage would be just the kind of thing that Roxy would have loved hearing about. We spent so much time talking about the tiniest details of our everyday lives. Discussing, analyzing, laughing. God, that was fun—and fun all the time. The silly minutiae. Do you realize how many embarrassing things you actually do every day? I miss having that with someone. Might be what I miss most. I could live with almost all the rest of the typical companionship difficulties if I still had that simple, dumb, everyday stuff with her. Maybe we should have spent more time talking about the big stuff. I'm all for talking about the big stuff now if she'd be open to it.

As pathetic as me not walking the dogs today was, she'd find a way to get a kick out of it. That positive life energy. But she broke up with me, so there's nothing I can do. I don't know if she thinks about those things, misses it. I shouldn't even think about her. She liked my weaknesses, at least for a while. I guess that's the period when love is blind—all the weaknesses and quirks are charming. Maybe women want to change men, or anyone wants to change anyone at least a little in a developing romance, but I didn't change for the better. She once said she loved me "not because I was perfect, but because of the things that made me not perfect." Maybe that was just in a card and she never actually said it, but it's stuck in my head as if it were an oath. I should go find it—no, that would be dumb. It's just a stock cliché. She probably never said it. If she did, I guess she never meant it.

The filth-filtered doses of air I suck in at Irene's apartment are the chemical opposite of a laughing gas, and it's getting to me—a depressing gas that makes you sad and lethargic, and a bad decision maker.

9:00 PM

I've opened Pandora's shoebox. I reached to grab a blanket in the back of my closet, and then—boom—that orange Nike box: letters, notes, cards. Wow, Roxy and I wrote to each other a lot in that first year, even though we saw each other at work almost every day. Writing by hand—we've lost it to e-mails and texts, and with it . . . permanence.

I shouldn't have looked at any of it. We sure were concerned about each other's feelings then, every thought. I found a funny one she wrote a few days after the first time I'd given her a tape with a couple of my songs on it. She hadn't said anything yet, and I was worried that she didn't like them. She handed me a card and asked me to read it later when I was alone. In it, she apologized for being selfish, but that hearing lyrics about another woman tossed her "like a rag doll in a clothes dryer," and her jealousy embarrassed her. It was very sweet. I knew we were in love. She did end up liking the songs, by the way. I wonder what she'd think if she read this thing.

In that box there were also letters from former students. The good-byes of every June were always sad. One kid, Sara, wrote, "Even though sometimes you were very conceited and too serious, you were the best teacher I ever had." Ha. I couldn't hide my true nature, I guess. She eventually became a teacher herself, first grade. She e-mailed me a photo of her desk at school a few years ago. She had my picture on it as her "inspiration." And she wonders why I was conceited?

Another, Coral, wrote, "I am your friend forever, Mr. Lucas. Money is not important. For me, what's most important is friendship without hypocrisy, and always speaking the truth—always. What you taught me."

These are fun to go through, but I have to shake my head—I'd never want these kids to know where I'm at now.

My favorite remark was written from a kid named Lester: "I'll always treasure my notebook from Room 208."

These should be good feelings, but sitting here knowing that the past was so much happier, holding the evidence of it in my hands, just—there's nothing good.

January 2, 12:00 PM

Randall is having an open house for Jazmine's apartment today. It's been going on for two hours, people stopping in front to read the sign, walking back and forth down the driveway to see the place.

"It's mostly couples who don't realize yet how small these bungalows are," he joked, as if he knew why Roxy hadn't moved in with me.

As the searchers go by my window, hearing the click of a woman's heels on the concrete driveway as she happily trots arm-in-arm with her boyfriend is like pulling hairs out of my head one memory at a time. It wasn't long ago that Roxy and I were that couple. There is nothing more exhilarating than looking at apartments together.

Danish philosopher Søren Kierkegaard said, "The most painful state of being is remembering the future, particularly the one you'll never have." It feels like everyone else's futures have been flashing past my kitchen window all day. People walk and walk and walk by, chatting about the square footage, the parking, the stove, the colors, the curtains, the rent. Such glee and hope, even the ones who are criticizing it, because they are doing something so happy—looking, exploring, moving, changing. There were a few single women, on whom Casino will undoubtedly (and smoothly) pounce. Some single dudes and gay couples. I just hope none of them have dogs.

I can't stand people moving in and me not moving out.

I remember when I first saw this place, I loved it. What a difference now. Nothing about it has changed, especially with its inhabitant, and that's why it's become this gray, stucco coffin. I can't wait until this open house is over and the gleeful are gone away.

3:00 PM

Damn, that sucked! I got over there, harnessed them up, told them we were going for a walk, and took them outside. We turned south on Hayworth and made it only about eighty feet before Lauren yowled like a fire alarm and bolted back up the street. Her leash ripped out of my hand. I stomped at the end of it but was a millisecond too late. Fortunately, Casino was walking down our driveway and heard me shouting. Seeing Lauren, he brilliantly dove on the ground, blocking the sidewalk with his body just as she got to him, and he grabbed her with his baseball-glove hands.

"What's going on?!" he asked as he nearly smothered the squirming, screeching Lauren in his arms.

"I tried taking these two dum-dums for a walk, and this is what I get."

"Is Irene home?" he asked.

"No, and there has been no word from anyone."

"Oh, wow, that's unbelievable."

"Seven days. I've been feeding these two all this time. I thought they might finally need some air. No more air, you two!"

What happened turned out to be exactly what I was afraid would happen. As much as I've dreamed of these dogs disappearing, it cannot occur on my watch. I thought I was holding the leashes tightly, but you know how sometimes when you hold something too tightly it slips from your grip?

Casino's shirt was damp. Apparently, he hadn't noticed in the excitement. "Damn, Casino, I think she peed on you. I'm so sorry."

"Oh, shit," he said. "What a day, and I'm late getting to the Valley."

"I owe you a silk shirt," I said. But I don't owe him a silk shirt. This wasn't my fault. I was just trying to get them outside so that I would have less to clean up inside. I took the dogs back in and closed the door. I'll go back there later to throw some dinner in the bowls. No more walks. Now I have to figure out where Casino shops.

January 3, 6:45 PM

I'm so embarrassed about yesterday. Am I a grown man? I couldn't handle walking two tiny Yorkshire terriers at the same time? Where was my focus? I'm going to try again, because I'm tired of cleaning up the urine-and-all a couple of times a day. And as you may have figured out, as I continue to clean a further path for myself and areas where they feed, I'm removing layer upon layer of dirt, and muck, and mud, and animal waste that is stomach turning and horrifying. But the percentages are changing. My clean area is growing against the dry-blob sediment. It's like unearthing Pompeii. Linoleum has truly earned my respect for having survived under this Vesuvius of putridity. As the white of my cleaned path rises, I feel as if I'm engendering change in something. If Irene comes home today, she'll see the original color of her floor in the cleaned parts. I wonder how she'd react?

What is a person thinking when she never cleans her floor, when she forces her own body to adapt to such horrendous conditions? The recovered patches might bother her. She might not want to think about what "clean" is and what it would mean for her, i.e., work, responsibility, maintenance, all the things that she has consciously given up. Is it depression? I don't know. But when I'm on my hands and knees cleaning the floor, and I look up to see the piles of bags and magazines, food containers, books, Yorkshire terrier calendars, and all of the things that she will not let go of, I know there's something overcast gripping her mind.

Can I blame her? Now that I'm on the inside, it makes sense that, after all she's been through, she sees nothing but darkness and misery. I've had a few rough months here, and my apartment's now a mess. I don't know when the last time was that I scrubbed my shower, for example. I wouldn't want a stranger in there. What if I were old and weakened like she is?

My dad had his stroke at sixty-six, just months after he'd retired. We thought it might mellow him out. But he'd lost the use of his entire right side from his jaw all the way down to his toes. It only made him more bitter. Then he had to battle colon cancer three times. But all the while, he maintained his patches of personal space impeccably—the area around the lamp near his chair, the end table next to his bed. The top of his dresser was perfectly clean and neat at all times. He also persevered against the cancer. As weak and uncomfortable as the surgeries and chemo made him, he never complained. His grousing ensued only if anything of his was out of its place—something left incorrectly in his area of the kitchen table, or his shampoo bottles in a different spot instead of set on his plastic seat in the shower. As I said, the stroke didn't soften him a bit. He bitched and moaned about everything else in life—the family, the bank, the city, the neighborhood, the price of milk—but never the cancer. The one thing to really bitch about would have been the cancer. Even in his final days the doctor marveled that my father never requested pain medication—no morphine, nothing. He needed a nursing home only for the last few weeks. When he passed away, no one in the family was able to get there in time. In response to a nurse who asked if she should call anyone in the family, he uttered what would turn out to be his final words on this callous earth: "Don't bother."

I think about him, Sheriff, when I'm at Irene's apartment. Even though she has damage from the brain tumor, she's in much better shape than my father was at the same age, yet she complains and complains about every little ache during the little spurts when I see her, every little issue with our landlord. And look at her surroundings. She does nothing to let herself have some happiness to look at inside below the level of those vases. It's just her own smog of blues. And the dogs, whom she says she loves, have been made gross. When I'm there, I feel as if I'm crawling around deep inside the gray, slimy passages of her brain, scrubbing one tiny area at a time. Maybe if I could have helped my father's depression and anger somehow, he could have had some OK years. But it was impossible to make him happy. Why would I be doing that for this stranger? And why not just deal with my own depression right now, by the way?

Irene claims to get companionship from these two dogs, but with the barking and the lack of training, I don't see how they can add enough positive to outweigh the negative that they do. I imagine her life in this apartment, which could be a sweet little place for a person like her, without those two dogs, clean and maintained. She could have a pleasant existence.

All this I get from the eight or so square feet of linoleum that I've cleaned up. I guess it's a ridiculous thought.

8:30 PM

Why am I sitting here like a B. F. Skinner lab assistant, developing behavioral theories around Irene and these dogs? I hate these dogs. I hate this situation. And it's sucking time and energy away from anything productive that might help me—as in me.

All I wanted from this dog log was help, peace and quiet. Now I have freakin' chores to do in taking care of those two. Working at home is a life of solitude. Having Roxy in my life, seeing her a few times a week, texting all day every day, I didn't feel alone. I didn't even think about it. And now suddenly that's all there is. I wish I could think about something else, but she's it. I'm constantly looking at my phone to check for her incoming anything. Even after five months, it's only intensified. I can't contact her because I'm the breakup-ee. Someone breaks up with you, they want you out of their life, and if you don't respect that, you're causing more problems. I have some pride. But pride is worthless. It's just sad and difficult, and painfully silent.

1:10 AM

I don't know what's going on in Roxy's personal life right now, but I'm assuming it has a great deal to do with a new pursuit of happiness. The idea that someone you love, your best friend, is making a concerted effort to replace you—your joys, conversations, your texts, your sex—is like a python squeezing all other thoughts out until your mind has only one purpose: to see the pictures that horrify you—an anti–Ludovico Technique for my Alex DeLarge (from *A Clockwork Orange*, Sheriff, you've probably seen it)—a therapy that disables aversion. I fill in the cavernous blanks because if I don't create answers of some kind, even fantasies that hurt me, then I'll have nothing but questions, rather than a place to focus feelings. The script ultimately needs moving pictures, and it's a horror film. All the phony first dates: "Do you like wine tasting?" "The Getty Museum has a *blah, blah, blah* exhibit coming that I'm so excited about," "Let's skip the gym and hike Runyon Canyon instead," "I just love how dominant the ocean sounds at night," "Your neck is so warm. What's that perfume?" "Oh, I probably shouldn't have another cosmo . . ."

I can't compete with new. I'm jealous of each unwrapped element of happiness that she discovers, and I wish them all failure. In Oscar Wilde's story "The Fisherman and His Soul," the fisherman says of the mermaid, "For her love I would surrender heaven." I've lost my heaven, or been cast out. Now, caught up in a net of my own bitter enmity, I'm actively picturing Roxy fighting with her whomever new man—I pray for it, for her feeling emptiness around her girlfriends, feeling desperate without our togetherness. And then my shame rolls whispering in like mist from the sea. All night, images unspool in unthinkably dark, flawlessly executed, punishing dreams. If envy is a sin, then I'm even sinning in my sleep.

2:20 AM

"Everything happens for a reason," Ally says.

"The condescension of that infuriates me, Ally, people telling you that there is a life lesson somewhere in all your pain. What a bunch of shit. I wish I could make them clean that up off of Irene's kitchen floor every day."

"I'm sorry. I don't know what the reason is, but you'll know it eventually. That's the beauty of growing through hard times. What are you doing still up?"

"I've learned my best life lessons from successes, not failures. The things that I've done well have brought me to the best people and the best situations. The failures have pushed me down, and people evacuate the area. Where I am—"

"That's where you grow. God, you used to be a poet. You used to see beauty in things. Write a song. Go read some Yeats and lighten up."

"Most poetry is sad, don't you know that? Failures give you lost time that you can never get back. And there is so much lost time. Are there life lessons for people starving in Africa, Ally? Are there life lessons for people being tortured in prisons around the world? It's bourgeois comfort talk, and you know better. I know people pay you to hear this shit, but they're people who already have enough money for therapeutic massage."

"Oh, well—fuck my whole life then."

I apologized. It didn't help.

Life is so seldom good. Most of the time it's painful and confusing. Loneliness is the worst poison of the human mind—so able to imagine better places, loving people, comfort and stability, just to emphasize the lousiness of whatever current situation.

And I can't just go "write a song." Music hurts. I haven't touched a guitar in at least five years.

Lauren is barking and barking over there.

I have been working on this poem though. It's about waiting— beauty and waiting—inspired by a Matisse painting Roxy and I both loved:

Zorah on the Terrace

With your nature's bliss,
You bathe yourself in
Timelessness,
Your porcelain fingers lift it
As water in a palm,
Cooling,
Spilling over your body,
Forever coming home.

Soft waves bring that to me
Always,
That somewhere sustained
Happiness,
That beauty of you
From which I drank,
Which may flow still,
As when I knelt on the tile,
We two, bathed in
Sapphire skylight,
My hand on your breast
As we kissed, and cleansed,
And whispered, and confessed.

There is no water
Without a shore,
No immersion, or totality,
Without the wonderful
Longing for air
And its answer in a kiss.

I am with Zorah on the Terrace,
She waits to Pray,
Or to be loved,

To be ravished,
Or to laugh,
To be listened to,
To Weep,
To hold,
Or be alone.

Beauty is never silent.

We listen, Zorah and I,
To the sky to catch the
Whisper of providence.

I hunger for you,
And, with you, all knowledge.

Zorah waits, unveiled,
Her eyes to me,
Her thumbs caress her satin tea
    gown,
I am breathless that her lips
May part and champion me.

Agonizing stillness.

And the constant rays yet drift
    west.

Might we forget
Our impossible solitude
With my prayer that it is tem-
    poral,
And that there is Infinity
In our kiss.

3:45 AM

I'm not going to send it to her.

4:00 AM

They say a sign of serious depression is not being able to put problems in perspective, and lists of little things become the focus of all your energy. But to accomplish that, one would need focus and energy. My heart is slowing like the final clicks of the Wheel of Fortune wheel as it lands on BANKRUPT. If I die tonight from beating myself up—I'm too tired to write a suicide note—let everyone just read this log if someone finds me. Ally can explain it.

I would take sleeping pills and get into a full bath. Cut a wrist to hurry the loss of consciousness, and then wait until I fall asleep and slide beneath the surface of life. The bathtub—Roxy's retreat. How I used to love to caress her underneath the surface. Maybe that's where I say good-bye.

January 4, 2:20 AM

Bang bang bang with these "holidays." Crushing. It feels as if all of the years have accordioned into one single, sour wheeze of notes that bend flat and are fading off. The entirety of activity during the day was feeding the dogs.

By tonight I'd had it. I wanted just to float. Away. To find out if I could fly, eternally, or could I finally just crater into the ground—eternally. I took myself to a weird karaoke place called the Orchid in Koreatown. It's where I knew I could float for a least a while. It's like a gaudy karaoke motel, not a bar so much, all separate rooms they rent by the hour. You're in there only with your group, so you don't have to lose any time listening to drunk strangers strangling "My Way"—you can strangle it your own drunk self. I went there alone, to sing, to scream. I was more alone than I'd ever felt, having been drinking Jack since 3:00, thinking of better days when I hadn't yet set my hand and footprints into the Walk of Failure.

"I would like a room, please."

"OK. How many in your party, sir?"

"One, and one ghost."

"Well, would you like to join another party? I can see if—"

"No, thank you. I'm fine. I'm practicing for a thing—"

"Oh, very good. Please follow me then to room 3."

Room 3 was empty, but the party had already begun. Red vinyl sofas, huge round coffee table in the middle with songbooks thicker than encyclopedias; streams of neon and LED lights pulsing like paparazzi; circular, convex mirrors everywhere reflecting dozens of tiny, flashing, distorted images of me and my gracious, bow-tied host. The front wall of monitors played videos of young Korean couples floating in canoes on lakes and walking on the sand on some Korean beach, the actors preening a perfectly impossible joy.

I checked the mic as if I were serious about the night, but had to laugh. The volume in these rooms is outdone only by the amount of reverb, which simulates the empty hull of an oil tanker.

I ordered a bottle of Jack Daniel's, and my host returned with something maybe Korean that was the same color, at least, with the added benefit of flame-thrower scorch that slashed its way down my esophagus with each hot and wooly swallow.

Karaoke always takes a few drinks to get started. I'm sure you know that. I can imagine a bunch of sheriff's deputies and their spouses blowing off some steam there. I lay down on a couch and let four random songs play through as my fiery fermented friend slowly cauterized the confluence of loss, anger, and self-loathing flowing beneath my skin.

I thought about what Ally'd said, and I wanted to sing with abandon, find the ecstasy in music the way I used to. Tonight, I wanted to do something associated with joy—if I could put my arms around it for one moment and feel it kiss me goodbye and say, "I love you, Richard." I don't want another year to suffer through. Or a night. Or worse, a day. Tonight has the weighted suggestion hanging around its neck that maybe it should be my last.

Have you ever been promised a promotion and not gotten it, Sheriff? Multiply that by a thousand concerts in arenas around the US and the world, and you'll know how I feel. I went there tonight to live with the past *that should have been.* I'd sing love songs and mean it with full-bore, unapologetic sincerity. I'd sing protest songs with righteous anger. I sang "Gimme Shelter." I sang "Jeremy." I sang "Fascination Street." I sang "Burning Down the House," "What's Going On." I sang "Waiting for a Girl Like You." I sang "Karma Police," "Rhinestone Cowboy," "Keep on Lovin' You," "Hello." I sang "Waterloo." I sang "Love Me Tender." I sang "I'll Stand by You." I sang "Sunday Bloody Sunday." I sang "The End." I sang everything as if they were my last words on this earth—glorious, self-pitying, ugly, lonely, exciting, drunker and drunker, and ecstatic.

This almost felt like the right time and right way to go out. I lay back down on a couch and prayed for it to come to pass through alcohol poisoning as loud, wordless music pulsed and spun around me. At closing, they peeled me off the vinyl and poured me into a cab.

I'm no better now, really, and already the blade of the hangover is chiseling away.

3:10 PM

I can't move without feeling like I'm going to puke.

This might be more maddening than when Irene was home, the way that Lauren barks all day. There's a new layer to it, added jabs of resentment. I get it. How did Irene show affection, just by feeding them? You can't touch them. Sometimes through the wall, I could hear Irene's voice, extra-high-pitched, calling them "the most beautiful doggies in the world," and asking them a series of questions about whether or not they realize that "they are the cutest doggies in the world?" I've even heard her singing—"There She Is, Miss America."

But does she touch them? Their hair is dry-soaked with that mud mix of urine, dirt, and horror through which it drags all day across the floor. *Drags?* They sit in it on the kitchen floor all day. If she touches them, how does she keep from becoming diseased? Has she developed some incredible immune system antibody superpower? Has she actually discovered a secret to longevity, an antidote against death? I get colds all the time. I mentioned I had that flu in early December, spent my few post-Sophie/pre-Lauren days with a fever—because I'm normal.

What is it that Lauren is longing for? Just Irene's voice? How low a bar of companionship has she? And Lauren does have Nelson with her. How come she can't just be happy to have him as her poop pal and let it be? The human she's been living with has actually been making her life worse. Come to think of it, Irene makes my life worse. *Bark.*

January 5, 1:20 PM

Midday. It was so cold last night that I slept with gloves on. Maybe I should go over there just so they can see a human being. I don't know. I already interrupt my day twice to go throw food at them, but now I'm thinking about, what, "visiting" them? Maybe I should try a walk again.

2:15 PM

Holy cow, those dogs have no idea what to do outside. They know to move up and down on the sidewalk well enough. Neither one darted away this time. But when I put them in the grass, they just stood there and looked up at me. Like putting an infant on a toilet seat. They didn't sniff around, didn't even lower their heads toward the blades. Nothing but empty stares.

I couldn't find a single patch of grass along our block that would interest them. Nor trees, nor bushes, nor walls, nor gravel, nor fences.

I thought that when dogs walk, they're out there following trails of scents, that they're supposed to be leaving their own scents behind, right? Like social or sexual messages to one another? Checking their e-mail. Swipes on dating sites, right?

Obviously, they'd already gone inside. But how can they be alive and not interested in what is happening on the rest of the canine planet? How can you knock that biology out of them? It was stunning to watch. And they don't know how to walk. They were either tugging ahead or sulking behind. Going left. Going right. No pace. Maybe they're not comfortable enough with me yet to behave like animals. What did they need me to do, pee on a tree to show them the process?

My mind is boggled. If they're never going to pee outside, that means that as I clean each area of the kitchen floor, they'll only mess it up again and again. There could never be a whole clean floor. If Irene comes home tomorrow, nothing will change, so why put in any effort?

That's another shock. Not a single soul has knocked on her door, nor on my door, to ask about what's going on. It's been ten days. Where are they? Bastards.

And, of course, as soon as I got the dogs back inside, Nelson peed on the refrigerator. That sneaky-as-a-U-boat little fucker was holding it in for when we came home. Amazing. Their olfactory senses must be so damaged that nothing can push their evolutionary buttons.

When the hell is Irene coming home? What is going on? Is this just because I live nearest to her? When did that become the rule? Casino's the one who was so friendly and charming with her. But that's the way with "charming" people. So skilled at dropping intense focus into tiny moments with people—so smiling and kind seeming, with the unflinching eye contact and shoulders and feet squared to yours, so willing to say nice things, always seem to like your shirt or your sunglasses, then they don't have to do anything else because people just think they're so freaking nice. I saw it with my father. It confused me so much as a boy to see how everyone outside of our family thought he was such a great guy.

I despise charmers—their compliments, promises—because little of it has even a tenth of a percentage of a chance of ever happening, i.e., being in touch, making plans, etc.

And this is a perfect example. Casino has asked me about Irene only one time. Not that I have any information on her—as if I were the information center of her life all of a sudden, which I'm not. But my no-information is information. I want to tell everybody that I have no idea what's happening, where she is, how she is, and that I'm getting screwed with these untended dogs next door. But this is exactly how it goes. Everyone disappears.

6:00 PM

Feeling a little better. Coping, I guess. Lauren is now refusing to eat. Strange since she's overweight and Nelson is as thin as a forced confession. I don't know what her eyes are telling me. I've tried to wait her out, but she just sits there by her food now like a nude model in a portrait class. She's smart. Sometimes she pretends to eat—grabs a few pebbles of the food and moves them around to get me off her back. Sometimes she drops several on the floor next to her bowl to make it look empty. If I leave her food there and come home, Nelson will devour it.

It makes me angry that she's playing this game. She wants to be fed when she wants to be fed, and only how she wants to be fed—and she wants me to read her mind. Well, Lauren, I'm not very good at reading the mind of the female, apparently of any species, so you shouldn't hold your breath. Do dogs know how to hold their breath?

Should I call animal services? Irene'd kill me, though it'd serve her right. Likely she'd never get them back. They might end up being put down. That would be a great scene, huh? *Old woman comes home from the hospital—slowly wobble-hobbling up to her front door, broken arm in a sling, fumbling for her keys with her left hand, looking for them through her one good eye, a slow curiosity drawing the smile at being home off of her face as the anticipated vibrations of the dogs behind the door is nothing but stillness streaming up to her one good ear.*

Yep, I want to be around for that moment when she gets inside and calls for her dogs and they don't come. I want to be here when she calls out to me, "Richard, where are my doggies?" Yes, I want to be the one to explain that I had them taken away, and "Oh, by the way, welcome home."

Maybe if I just go over there to talk to them for a few seconds. Through my mask? And about what? That I have no idea what's going on with Irene or when she's coming back? About what verminous, miserable, little untrained rats they are? I'm losing it.

January 6, 10:30 AM
First thought of the day: what abject misery waits for me over there? I guess I'll go and check in on them.

11:20 AM

Got over there. Two fresh ponds of pee. Cleaned them up, also expanded my cleaner area of the kitchen floor. Best move would be to just buckle down and do the whole thing, lessen the weight of the stench, if I can. Don't know. When is she coming back?

That was enough of a visit. I'll go back later. The dogs do seem to be a little less frantic at my arrival. It's amazing how they get used to a stranger. Why is that? I'm showing them no kindness or tenderness, no affection. Why would they look like they care about me? There's nothing there, you stupid dogs. Just stop peeing all over the place.

January 7, 11:20 AM

I had a meeting with a graphic design agency this morning, a "creative staffing" place. I have to get more work. They place you into freelance positions at a prenegotiated rate, then take 10 percent. The rate is way less than I can charge on my own, but it's been so slow that I have no one to charge my rate to.

I haven't done on-site freelancing for several years. I hate it. Grunt work. Early on, I spent six months at a studio in Santa Monica placing and proofing ingredients lists and nutrition panels, as per FDA regulations, onto Hughes Markets' entire line of home-label generic products. You're picking up files that ten other people have already tinkered with, taking orders from obsessive production managers who only know time and not creativity, as much as there can be in tweaking text kerning and the box outline stroke weight of a standardized ingredients panel.

I think the meeting went well, professional. It gave me a reason to shower and use the iron. I have to wait for them to decide if they're going to take me on. The guy said he'd let me know within a week or so. I went over to Irene's. Fed the dogs. We walked, no progress. Cleaned a little.

8:15 PM

Stasya just told me she's moving. Goddamn it. Her husband is having more trouble breathing, and they think it's because of the paint dust from Pristine Automotive, the auto body place on Fairfax on the other side of our block.

"Are you sure?"

"Yes. He says so," she said with sad eyes. Then she shrugged, "It's OK. It's OK."

"It's not OK. I can't stand this."

She laid her hand on my shoulder. "Don't worry about anything, my Richard," she said. "You are young. You have love."

"No, I don't—"

She touched her chest. "In here you do. That's more important than anything outside."

I hugged her.

"Roxy will come back to you. You are a good man."

"Thank you. I want you to come back to me, too."

"You will see. Love always wins. She will come back."

Even in leaving, Stasya gave me hope. Are you married or divorced or anything, Sheriff? If you're anywhere near my age, which likely you are, you've dealt with heartache. That's a shitty fact of life.

Everyone leaves. That's a shitty fact of life, too. I'm slowly figuring out how my father was affected by, born into actually, an abandonment complex. I don't know if there's any such thing, but he knew that people can and will leave you without warning—and for good. It became part of his DNA. He passed that DNA on to me. I have all of the logic about it, yet here I sit in a situation with Roxy where I'm waiting and hoping for a solution. I'm like Jacqueline Kennedy climbing over the back of that motorcade convertible, grasping for the pieces of JFK's skull. It has to be those broken pieces put back together—nothing else—so I can believe that abandonment isn't a permanent law, that it's fixable.

In the meantime, you hope and cope. When someone leaves you, if you still love them, then you hope, hope that they'll change their mind and come back. Maybe it's part of the chemistry of denial, but hope can keep you breathing.

When someone you love dies, you don't have hope, because you have reality. You go into coping right away. But in relationships, when that former partner is still out there somewhere, you just can't help but hope. Hope is high and cope is low—you drag yourself through each day thinking round and round about what she's thinking: *Does she think about me at all? What is she feeling? Does she have any regret about ending it? Thoughts about me?*

But as time goes on, if there's no communication, or if there's negative news between the two, then hope fades. That's when "cope" can finally begin to rise, you see? You have a limited amount of thoughts to use in one day. And when coping thoughts do come, they allow you to imagine your life forward. It's very difficult for me to get there because I want to conquer that abandonment via the abandoner. The cycle of wanting to hold onto and fix that event to maintain one's own ego and self-respect begins.

So I don't feel good being alone, and I guess I fear abandonment—through my father's experience—when I'm with someone. DNA. If I could just get better at being alone. Friends don't count. It's intimacy that's the narcotic. And unfortunately, intimacy is something that some people can fake very well, or they're skilled at having it and then being able to throw it away for whatever reason—they get scared, they get bored, they want another victim.

I fear people in Los Angeles. Destroying others is like a quick high from a whip-it if you have no empathy whatsoever. I don't know. Maybe I'm mixing things up with sociopaths or narcissism. But how does one find a non-narcissist in this town? We're all people who were able to chuck everything—walk away from all we knew and the people we loved, and who loved us—to move here to chase thin fantasies. We begin our new lives in Los Angeles only after having abandoned everyone without pity.

Do you have pity? I'm sure they try to train law enforcement officers not to have feelings either way, because that'd get in the way of procedure. Or maybe they train you to be human beings? Otherwise you'd be helpless against becoming a sociopath with all that power. I'm sure you're not. I could be. Couldn't we all turn?

How do malicious armies arise out of ordinary citizenry time and time again throughout history?

By the way, I'm not a sociopath.

I told myself that if I get any call about work or from that agency, that I'd walk the dogs an extra time today. No call, but I might do a night walk anyway.

January 8, 6:30 PM

I don't know why I hadn't thought of this earlier, but I finally found a simple use for all of the newspapers that Irene has piled up. After I feed them tonight I'm going to lay a few down over the areas of the floor that I've cleaned so that I'm not cleaning the same spots over and over like Lady Macbeth trying to clean her bloody hands. This could make my mornings much quicker. I'm so damn excited, I may not be able to sleep tonight.

January 9, 11:30 AM

Waiting to hear from that freelance agency. It's possible they won't even call if they don't want me. People in this town are all so skilled at making you feel spectacular while you're in the room. It doesn't mean anything with regard to their decision on you. They say great things to make themselves feel powerful as they watch your face light up with found dignity. It must feel wonderful to make someone feel that good.

I'm waiting to get something that I don't even want, but I need the work. I do have a presentation meeting tomorrow with the anesthesia consultants group, but beyond that it's just a trickle.

Lauren just will not eat. Her bowl is near a pillow I'd set down with a towel on it, and her new ploy is to get a corner of the towel in her teeth, drag it over and then lay it on top of her bowl in protest. Absolute smartest damn thing I've ever seen. But, I have to confess, I get really pissed. I yell. Little girl dog sitting there shaking like an electric razor—I feel like an asshole, but she can be such a jerk. All I'm trying to do is feed her. And she's an animal. Isn't eating priority number one in the animal kingdom? In fact, that's precisely what I was asking her in my shouting. Didn't get an answer, just the eyes.

I took them out for a walk to see if some time away from the bowl and some invigoration might make her hungry. But walking them only invigorated my own frustration. It is so crazy watching them not go to the bathroom outside. That incredulity on their faces when I tell them this is their time to do it, that it's the right thing to do. It's an alien concept to them, spoken in words they've never heard strung together in that order before.

We passed by a young, attractive woman, very fit in her yoga pants and tank top, walking her little fluffy white dog along like Athena guiding a cloud. As the three dogs stopped to sniff one another, I asked if she could get her dog to pee in the grass to show these two dum-dums what's supposed to be happening. Yep, that's me with women, Sheriff—I always know just the right words to say. I'd also forgotten that I was wearing latex gloves and had a surgical mask hanging around my neck. And, of course, the two mangy, sad Yorkshire terriers make me look like Man of the Year.

The only way for me to get myself to touch these dogs with my naked hands would be to wash them. But what use would it be to bathe them and then set them down on the dirty floor? Their hair is so long (and I've learned that it's not fur, it's hair) that it scrapes against the floor. It's no use to clean them. I wish I could cut all that hair right off. But I'm so frustrated that there's very little space between my wanting to help them and my going Sweeney Todd. Would I leave the meat pies for Irene in her freezer where Sophie was so ignominiously laid to rest, the way he would? Yes, I would.

All this rushes through my head before I choke out to the girl, "These . . . aren't . . . my dogs. I'm . . . taking care of them . . . for my neighbor. . . . She's . . . an older lady, and . . . and is . . . she's in the hospital." I was speaking so haltingly and, I know, still in the habit of gripping the leashes as if they were a rope from a rescue helicopter, that I'm sure it only corroborated her assumption that I was criminally insane. My throat dried as I said the words "taking care of them." Saying it to another person made it real.

Yoga Pants squirmed in her cuteness—which actually made her cuter. She and her little Larry Tate dog didn't like the dum-dums.

"Well, have a nice afternoon," I said as I pulled us all away. I should have said I'd been painting my apartment. Why do I always think of the right thing to say when it's too late? I turned and shouted, "Hey," as I held up my hands, "I'm just in the middle of painting my apartment. That's why the gloves and the mask." She turned her head and gave me a pursed-lip nod and quickened her athletic pace away. I doubt she'll be walking her dog on Hayworth Avenue anymore. Fate? Fatal?

Got them inside. Lauren still refused to eat. I decided to leave the food in the bowl and let whatever's going to happen happen. Maybe Nelson will gain some weight and Lauren will lose some. I've lost a few pounds now. I won't be the only one deteriorating with the stress. I laid down a square of newspaper and am hoping for the best.

January 10, 11:00 AM

I just got a text from Roxy. Totally out of the blue. Just two words: "Ubiquitous Zigzags." That was one of our funny little phrases we used to send each other whenever either of us saw an Art Deco building around town.

We'd been to an architectural symposium put on by the Los Angeles Art Deco Society at the Egyptian Theater. Then later we took a fun tour of the old Art Deco buildings and landmarks downtown. The guide kept on saying, "And, of course, once again, you see the ubiquitous zigzags" with every design he discussed, and we'd try to keep from laughing. Zigzags are elemental in Art Deco stylings. Once you know that, you notice them everywhere in L.A.

Goddamn it, I miss her.

I don't know what to think. These tiny bits of communication, and now a text that, to me, recalls how connected we were, right? Intended to make me smile? It has—but what the hell? She's clearly thinking of me. It can't just have been a spontaneous accident of fondness, merely temporal. It's a message. She's warming up. Her resentment, or anger, or disappointment, or whatever it was might be softening. This is fantastic. And it's funny. She still has a sense of humor about us. This is excellent. What should I do? Ubiquitous zigzags!

12:30 PM

I just texted her back. I did what either of us always used to do. I bounced the same words back. When we were together, these funny little things meant *I love you* and *I love you, too*. I sent it. "Ubiquitous zigzags." It took me an hour and a half, but I did it. Excellent!

3:30 PM

Three hours and she hasn't responded. I don't know what the hell this is. Am I supposed to do something? What I do have to do is get myself together for the anesthesia group meeting at 5:00. I did somehow knock out some ideas to show them. Maybe I'll be able to pocket some propofol on my way out.

January 11, 5:00 PM

Walking and feeding. No peeing or pooping. They are getting used to me and this routine. Not tugging at the leashes so much. Damn it, it's a routine already. Nelson prances sometimes, both hind legs at once, then both front legs. Kind of cute. And he's always sniffing, trying to sneak scraps that he finds into his mouth. I don't let him. He allows me to grab his mouth and open it gently until whatever chicken bone or piece of fast-food wrapper he's chewing on falls out. He looks straight into my eyes with a sense of guilt, being caught, but obedient. I tap him lightly on the nose, he grabs my finger with his teeth, and we shake on it.

Still cleaning in kitchen.

January 12, 9:20 AM

Woke up early, and I realized that the dogs wake up pretty early, too. So, I went and fed them, cleaned a little more of a path. I may be able to walk in there without bags over my shoes soon. It smells so bad in the morning. The night holds the bacteria in a headlock until daybreak when it says *uncle*. And, of course, the dogs always leave me something to clean up. The 409 is surface cleaning, but it doesn't do anything for the smell. How could it if it's in the rugs, the furniture, every crack and crevice in the place? I got there early today, but they'd still already crapped in the living room. How early would I have to wake up to beat them to the pooping? I don't feel like doing that, but cleaning up every morning is nothing to look forward to.

January 13, 10:00 AM

Still waiting to hear from that freelance agency. Makes for a long day, but my hopes are still up. I need work. People always say "Think positive." So vacuous. How could any of my thoughts sitting here in my apartment affect the decision that the agency is making today or made yesterday or will make tomorrow? Vibrations or something that makes an impact. Is that how people and businesses make decisions—waiting for mysterious oscillations from miles away? What am I supposed to think positively about? Cleaning up after these two damn dogs every day, and breathing through a painter's mask? Plus, my damn girlfriend broke up with me and won't even talk to me outside of a two-word text. You have a good job, Sheriff. You have a pension, health benefits, etc. I'm sure that your wife finds a sense of security from that. I don't even offer those things to myself, let alone to a mate. I promise that as soon as I find the positive thing to think about, I will try to think about that thing very positively. I'll let you know.

1:00 PM

Fed the dogs. No word about Irene. Where would word come from? I've never seen a visitor over there.

No word about work.

2:30 PM

OK, I found some positive things. Ready? I'm not in terrible health. Other than some facial rosacea that I have to medicate every day, and acid reflux disease, which I'm supposed to take a pill for every day, and prematurely graying hair, which I blame on Irene, my bad knee, the stupid shingles, and a family history of colon cancer and stroke, I have my health. I'm not bedridden, except when hungover, and I have all of my mental faculties—too many, even. So that's positive. With the rosacea, in fact, I actually touched my face up with a little makeup before the meeting with the agency both to cover it up some, which I normally do, but also to try to hide the dark circles under my eyes from all the lack of sleep.

It makes me feel self-conscious when I worry that someone would be able to see that I'm wearing foundation. I can't stand the rosacea, and it's worse when I'm stressed. But when I touched up the dark circles, I think it made the area under my eyes look too light, and I might've looked weird. But I felt I had to do it, because who wants to start to work with someone who looks like they were just dumped out of a coffin? I used some tanning lotion, too, before the meeting. Because of the rosacea, I can't spend any time in the sun without it getting really red and bubbling up a little bit.

Another positive would be that I'm good at graphic design. My work is received well. Roxy thinks I'm great at it, wishes I didn't hate it. About one in ten jobs are things that I actually enjoy thinking about and designing. I have no motivation or "dreams" invested in graphic designing, though. Every time the phone rings and it's a new graphic design job, it's another shovelful of dirt cleared to make my grave because it's not the phone call or e-mail that I want. What is that call? I don't even know anymore. It used to be a new manager, or a club, or a record company.

Time has gone by so fast, I don't know what I want. If I were a better businessman, an actual interested entrepreneur, then maybe I would pull in a little more business and some money would help me feel better. If I wasn't driven crazy for so long by those dogs, I might have been able to figure things out these last couple of years, instead of just losing a girlfriend and work. And now I have to tend to these dogs a few times a day, so everything is interrupted, even the interruptions. But there—my graphic design work is another positive to think about today.

Other than that, I think you're supposed to think about the people who love you, be appreciative and grateful for that. My family loves me. None of them have expressed that they don't. It's not incorrect to go on under the assumption that family members begin with a love for you that must be sullied to be lost. My father and mother are gone. I'm not sure they count. In many ways it's a positive that I don't have to deal with my father anymore. A miserable man, made more miserable by those health complications. Worst part of that might have been that my mother left him before he got home from the hospital after the initial stroke. She'd had it, rightfully so, and wasn't going to spend her late years caring for an uncaring man. I understand that now, but it devastated me at the time.

Abandonment. More of it. Again. Bookended late in life. I fear that happening to me in my old age. What I'd thought about Roxy was an assurance that'd never be. But I won't be my father. Not having to deal with him anymore is a burden lifted, so a positive, except that, genetically speaking, it pretty much spells out that I have a titanic stroke to look forward to.

My siblings are spread out across the country. We're not in very good touch, except Ally and me, so we're able to avoid most conflicts. I don't have the burden of kids' birthday parties, or graduations and shit. It's not that we don't want to talk, I don't think, but we each choose to play it safe and distant, less hearing and giving unsolicited advice and crap like that. The times when I do see people for weddings, etc., it remains relatively peaceful and polite until someone insinuates that I've thrown my life away—asks about retirement plans, IRAs, owning a house—and then I get pissed and drink more. But that doesn't happen too often, so that's a positive.

There, I just put in a solid thirty minutes of thinking positive. That ought to do some good in "the universe." The deranged people in Southern California say "the universe" more frequently than "hello" or "thank you." Ally, too. Yes, I am cynical, or, I guess, specifically, becoming agnostic about there being a specific God who sees and hears all, who works miracles—yet at the same time allows people to suffer so—or who has never not given power to so few over so many. But I'm even more skeptical about a "universe"— something that is a chemical accident from millions of years ago, expanding beyond our knowledge of science and imagination—that somehow this nonhuman energy entity has power, thoughts, and an ability to affect our lives when we put thoughts and desires out "to" it. "Universe" people scoff at the idea of any God being omnipotent, but they just as easily pontificate that the "universe" is out there listening, acting, planning, and reacting. Where is this universe for me? Why is mine so tiny, pale, painful, so mired down in failure by these dogs and Irene? I would compare my universe to almost anyone else's to show them that it—if it exists not just as an element of science—is not a friendly quasi-deity worthy of trust or admiration or hope. And yet I do pray once in a while.

It's a sunny afternoon. That's a positive thing. I'm going to go over and check in on the dogs and walk them, because it would be "positive" for me to not have to clean up shit after them at dinnertime.

January 15, 6:00 PM

Two days walking and feeding. No appropriate peeing or pooing. Still cleaning. Nothing from Roxy. Nothing on work. Nothing on Irene.

January 16, 10:35 AM

When I went over there this morning, they'd already peed and pooped, and I was tired from bad dreams, so I just fed them and left. Why do I have so many dreams about Roxy? I dreamed that I could hear her on the phone having a teasingly sexy conversation with her new boyfriend, if she even has one, which I certainly don't know. It was torture, yet I kept listening. Truly, since it was my dream, I was writing the dialogue for the two happy-faced new lovers. Why would I do that? Why can't we control the content of our dreams? Ally told me to write the dreams down, which I'm not doing, but that one knifed me pretty good, so I guess I did just write it down.

I know it's part of the spontaneity of being human that we're victims to the pounding subconscious for a third of our hours, but if someone could invent a way that we could guide our sleep-selves into joyous nighttime revelry, the increase of worldwide happiness would be exponential. There must be a pill. There are so many pills, antidepressants, anti-anxieties—why not thought-pills for the night?

I don't know what those dogs dream about. If Nelson or Lauren do have bad dreams, they couldn't be worse than what they awaken to.

I know that I said I'd walk them if I heard good news about any work, but I haven't heard anything, and I'm sick of thinking about it, so I'm going to go over there anyhow.

2:00 PM

It finally happened—Lauren peed outside! So suddenly—and it seemed so simple. We were coming back down Hayworth from Romaine. I was frustrated as ever when she just stopped and peed against a wall. Didn't sniff or anything. Then she looked up at me as I said, "Wow—good girl! Good girl! That's what I've been insisting on all this time! You figured it out. Now you won't have to go inside and be disgusting!" I don't know if she gave a shit at all about what I was saying. Nelson stood there looking at us with his head tilted fifteen degrees and his tongue hanging out of the left side of his mouth. (That just started to happen. I think he lost a tooth.)

January 17, 12:00 AM

It's midnight. I just got back after a late-night walk with them. A couple of weeks after I first moved in here Irene had a very bad black eye. She told me she had been mugged at 5:30 in the morning while on a long walk. She claims that she used to walk three miles every morning. Maybe she was talking about before the tumor. But the black eye was real, Casino saw it. Luckily, it was the eye she doesn't use. She claimed that a guy tried to rob her at gunpoint and hit her in the face with the handle of a gun. She was only out there with the two dogs, no purse or anything. Seemed a strange story. I have a feeling now that she'd fallen, and it was a cover. I get that. I've seen her drive; I don't think she has the ability to see or move in a straight line.

It's a long stretch between dinnertime and breakfast. Late at night, I feel like I can hear them breathing over there, looking up into the darkness wondering where Irene is, where their normal, as it were, life is.

I walked them for the first time at night. They seem to appreciate the cool air against their faces. They trot, and I follow more than lead. Nothing comes of it. Even though Lauren had peed that one time, their habits are still the same. Failure.

At least it gave me something to do. Plus, I put new bulbs in Irene's front room light, the chandelier. So many days I just sit here waiting for Roxy to call, wondering why she isn't. The way she said that "I love you, Richard" on the last day. It sounded like an accusation, as if it were something that I wouldn't understand—that she loved me more than I could imagine, and that imbalance consumed the joy in it all. Has that ever happened to you, Sheriff? I think there should be a rule in breakups that if you are the one calling for it, you can't tell the other person that you love them because that lingers for a long, long time. It might be unbreakable.

Much better is to tell the person, "I don't love you anymore, Richard." If Roxy'd told me that, it would've hurt but helped me maybe.

All these months we haven't spoken. I didn't know that Breakup Bags was going to be my only chance to tell her that I still loved her and that I wanted to work things out. And I've been waiting. Walking these stupid dogs gives me at least a distraction. The sad thing is, she was great with animals—as good as she was with the troubled kids at school. I wonder what she would've done in this situation. She wouldn't have been able to stand the contamination at Irene's, but I don't think she would be able to look at the dogs in that pitiable situation and not do something about it. Plus, she loves to clean. Anyway, thinking about her has done me absolutely no good. Waiting for someone who is not going to come is a terrible, senseless, explainable anguish. But I can't let go of what I thought our life was going to be—someday a house, laughter all the time, bottles of wine, stupid TV shows—tidings of comfort and joy, comfort and joy. The way that it ended so suddenly has left all the days ahead of me empty.

Then again, future-wise, I took out my retirement from my seven years of teaching to finance my album. Stupid. Gone.

I make the same plan over and over if she and I were to talk: what I would say, how I'd behave, what I'd need to hear her say— start a process of reconciliation. I feel very mature and proud when I think about those things, but Roxy can't see it. Then again, I don't know what she sees. Mutual friends tell me they don't know what she's thinking. She won't talk about us. So all I can do is look at her actions, which I know very little about, except that she does not contact me. If she does, I'm ready. This time I want to get married.

There—I said it. I should have said it to her. Should have said it to her. Why hadn't I? I'm an idiot—I'm not supposed to be thinking about her, or waiting, yet I have an exact way in my head that the two of us could be married, probably in six months: 1) Talk, 2) Reconcile, 3) Plan, 4) Move in, 5) Marry.

See that? Typical. I put "Plan" in there at number 3. That's me subconsciously buying time, implanting hesitation. Change it to a four-point plan, damn it.

I've had too much wine. You want a confession, Sheriff? You're getting it all out of me tonight. I'm ashamed of what I'm about to tell you, but I have to tell someone. It's not all shame. Part of me is proud of it. But the shame is how silly I am, how love-blind that I've been through this breakup.

Here it goes—I needed a battery for my watch, a beautiful, bold, black-and-white Swiss Army diving watch that Roxy gave me several years ago that I love. I'd still been wearing it, even though it had been frozen on 7:15, as a reminder to get it taken care of. Most of the time, however, it only made me think that it was 7:15. It was Friday evening last week. I'd just had a really positive meeting with that anesthesia client. It generated a bunch of new ideas, and so I thought I'd picked up enough new work to make it through a month, maybe two. I know I should've mentioned some good news to you, finally, but you'll soon see why I didn't. Plus, that client called and canceled all the new stuff on Monday, so it's gone anyhow. But the thought of some real income that night, plus the existence of Roxy's "ubiquitous zigzags" text that morning, had me on a momentarily positive zig.

On the way home, I stopped at Wanna Buy a Watch?, the store on Melrose just east of La Cienega, to get a watch battery. Very cool place, if you haven't been—vintage jewelry, watches, that stuff. It was actually higher-end than I'd anticipated, so I was embarrassed that all I wanted was a seven-dollar battery. A very appealing, retro-attractive woman—midforties, red hair, curves like Mulholland Drive—approached me. She was dressed perfectly for the store: red heels, black fishnets, pencil skirt, vintage cardigan (three buttons undone, the lowest touching the tail of the orange kitten embroidered on it). With her fresh cherry smile, she asked how she could help. I was a little disappointed that she didn't ask if I wanted to buy a watch. She had a flower pinned behind her left ear that smiled as warmly as she did. I told her about my watch, and she said that she'd have to take it to the back, so it would be a few minutes.

"Feel free to look around," she said with the confident coyness of knowing I'd already looked around her.

The collection they sell there is incredible. It reminded me of Roxy, because she loves vintage jewelry. Necklaces, bracelets, watches that would have looked amazing on her. And then there were rings—a lot of stones I don't know anything about—and then diamonds. One ring in particular practically smashed through the glass at me. It had three stones across the top, and a very cool pattern of zigzag lines that made up the base, silver, gorgeous—Art Deco. I never really thought about diamond rings, but now I was looking at one that was a perfect match for someone I loved. My heart filled with virile madness and an unstoppable tear blurred my vision. I pulled it together because I didn't want to be an emotional wreck when the saleslady returned with my working watch and seven-dollar fee.

In a moment, I smelled the light fragrance of her flower, "Would you like to see anything?"

"No, I'm fine," I said trying to unshake my voice. "You've got amazing stuff here."

"Is there someone special that you're shopping for?"

"I'm not really shopping, just browsing while I waited."

"I've been in this business for a long time," she said. "And men don't browse at diamond rings unless they're in love." She turned the key and opened the case. "I'm Valerie. I bet it's the Art Deco you're liking. It's vintage 1930s," she said as she slipped it onto her little finger. "It's very small though, too small for me, unfortunately."

"Don't tell me it's a 4½."

"So there is someone special," she smiled. "Lucky for her, it's a 4½."

My heart hammered as if it were breaking down a door, but the adrenaline felt good.

So, this is how it feels, I thought. I'd never come close to this kind of clarity about being a man. The sense of commitment warmed my blood like a shot of bourbon after a swim in a cold lake. I could share my life, be part of a family with someone, a true partner. Valerie continually rotated her hand ever so gently against the light, bewitching the diamonds into a captivating aurora borealis.

This is the perfect ring for the perfect person at the perfect moment, I thought. *I could do this.*

"You're so in love. I can see it in your eyes. It's very sweet," she said.

"But she's not in love with me, unfortunately."

"Are you sure? I find that very hard to believe," she said.

She was good, very good.

"We were together for seven years—"

"Seven?"

"Yeah, that's my fault. She ended it a few months ago. The trouble is, I think it was because she thought I wasn't committed enough."

"Then where did the seven years come from?"

"Well, I wanted to work it out, but she doesn't seem to, so—"
But *ubiquitous zigzags*, I thought. *All of life is ubiquitous zigzags.*

"Yet here you are looking at the perfect ring," she said.

This was a life moment—a long time coming—but finally facing me now.

"Yes," I said, gathering my external self, "but not at the perfect time. I think it's too late, unless she calls or something to show she wants to work on it. This is crazy for me to be standing here looking at this." *Crazy, yes, but the best feeling I'd ever had.* "I need to step away."

"I think all she needs is for you to show her how much you love her," she said.

I heard the courage of my mother in those words. I was in a hyperextended spiritual universe of masculinity and femininity, surrounded by flowers atop the peak of a mountain where two people come together to unite forever at the very edge of the space.

"That's truly all a woman ever asks for."

That punched me in the teeth. I smiled. "But she didn't ask for that. She ended the relationship. There's a difference. It wasn't an ultimatum. It was a decision."

"You think so much like a man," she answered. "This isn't a mathematical calculation or a game plan for a basketball team. These are emotions. This is love. If you were together for seven years, then she truly loves you, and she will for the rest of her life, no matter what. If you give her this ring, she'll know everything she needs to know."

This woman, Sheriff, wants me to buy an engagement ring for my ex-girlfriend.

"That would be insanity," I said. "I've left her alone. We've only talked once, and she didn't respond to that as I'd hoped. I came in here for a new battery because mine is dead. Do you have it? To suddenly show up and give her an engagement ring is the stuff of a restraining order. What would she tell people as she wore it around town? *Oh, this?—Richard, my ex-boyfriend, gave it to me a few months after I broke up with him.* How embarrassing for me."

She probably could get a restraining order on me for that, right, Sheriff?

"There's nothing more beautiful than giving a woman you love a special ring like this," Valerie insisted. "If she doesn't want to consider it an engagement ring, you can simply tell her that the years you had together were something that you treasure and that this ring is a symbol of that love and how special she will always be to you."

How I wish that could work—one giant, enormous, sweeping, all-encompassing gesture of commitment to fix it all in the grasp of a moment, something I should have done two, three years ago, at least, that could give me the future that I've been missing. Maybe in a novel or a romantic movie, but in real life, it was a few steps across the river from romance toward lunacy.

But the three prisms of dancing diamond dreams were hypnotizing me.

Is this just my typical commitment-phobic way of thinking? I thought. *Always finding a reason to do the same non-thing? But wait, I don't have a commitment problem. She does. She's the one that ended it. I wanted to work on it, right? But maybe she only wants to work on it if there is a commitment from me. She did text me.*

"You can put a deposit on it, and we'll hold it for you for sixty days—two months. That way you can think on it, and it will still be here," Valerie explained, as if that would be a perfectly non-insane thing to do.

If I don't tell anyone about it, it won't feel so pathetic, I thought. And that was that.

"Let's do it," I said, and I handed her my credit card, my heart, and my secret. I was about to get a decent-sized check. I couldn't leave that ring to rest on another woman's hand. I made an actual decision, one that could last for sixty days, or forever. Valerie looked at me as if I were a lumberjack who'd just come home from a hard day's work and wanted his dinner hot, delicious, and in front of him on the kitchen table right after we throw everything off and fuck on it. I believe that her breasts heaved. All I would lose would be $400, and now there's a sense of a deadline on this thing. If Roxy doesn't come around within the two months, then it's over. There's surety in that.

We added the battery to the charge, and I left.

It was actually 7:15, and in a minute, it would finally be 7:16.

The thoughts of those diamonds drilled through my head like a strip miner setting explosives.

The deposit was probably stupid to do, Sheriff. It certainly doesn't make me think about Roxy less, and it makes the loss deeper with a sparkling symbol on top. Well, she'll never know. Only Valerie and I—and you. I wonder what Valerie will think when the sixty days are up and I haven't returned, as she takes the ring off "Hold" and puts it back up for sale.

"He should have done what I told him to do," she'll mutter. "Too bad."

All romance is dead.

January 17, 6:30 PM

Walking and feeding. Lauren peeing. Nelson eating grass. Still cleaning. Kitchen floor getting there. It's disgusting.

January 18, 11:10 PM

I took the dogs on two fruitless walks today. But concerning tonight's walk, I asked Casino to do me a simple favor. It's Saturday, and I had an invitation to a party. I thought I'd try being at a social gathering. This would be the first night that I haven't been here to walk the dogs. I asked Casino if he'd do it for me. Casino's a sweet guy and is not one to refuse a little favor. He loves doing favors because he's never hesitant to remind you of what he's done for you lately. I think he's got a quid pro quo notebook. He finds the sneakiest ways to drop in favor reminders at unsuspecting moments that make you think, *He's still thinking about that?* For example, in the middle of a fun debate about, say, an athlete's bad temper, he'll throw in a line like "What he needs to do is to cool off. Remember that time when I helped you install your air conditioner? I cut my finger pretty bad doing that, too, I think, right?"

I don't think society should have to function on a mandatory counterbalance of kindness. Maybe that's the way Irene had been weighing the barking—that since I'd done nothing for her, why should she do anything for me? Yes, why? How do you change a person like that?

So I asked Casino—could he please walk the dogs later on, the night walk? Reluctance tightened his face, but he said he'd do it—after all, this is the jackpot of favor debt.

"It'll be fine," I assured him. "Just wrap the leashes around your wrist and fingers. And if you don't feel like picking up after them, don't worry about it. It'll be dark, no one'll see." I knew that was foremost in his mind. It had been a huge hurdle for me, bagging that stuff. If he gets caught and gets the fifty-dollar ticket, that's his problem. I'll just owe him an even bigger favor then.

The party sucked. Half the people there knew Roxy, but no one mentioned her name. So uncomfortable. The thought that she'd show up had me panicked. Alone or with a guy, it would kill me to see her as an independent, not-smiling-with-me person. But I also stressed about why she wasn't there. *Was she somewhere more exciting, with someone more exciting? Does she want to avoid me?* I shouldn't have gone. This anxiety was just what I'd feared. My eyes were darting everywhere, trying to read people's thoughts, watching the front and back doors. I drank a bottle of wine myself, left early, and went home.

Casino stopped me in the driveway as I arrived. He wasn't his usual bubbly self. *Can't be good.* "Hey, Casino, how's it going?" I said, trying to change my assumption.

"Not good," he said. "I don't know how to tell you this, but—one of the dogs ran away."

Boom.

"Which one?" I asked. I don't know why I asked that, as if it would matter.

"I don't know which," he said. "I can't tell them apart, and I don't know their names."

I understood his defensiveness. They're not his dogs, and the first move is to blame them anyhow. I get that.

"OK, can I please have Irene's keys back?" I said. "I'll go see which one's there."

He followed me to her door. *How could he have screwed this up so badly? Then again, Lauren had gotten away from me, too.*

"We have to figure something out," I said, as I unlocked the screen door and waves of dread along with it. "What do people do when they lose a dog? Who do we call?"

I was saying "we" because I wasn't going to let him out of this.

Then, as I pushed my key into the deadbolt lock, I heard barking. I stopped. My head drooped against the door.

Oh no, not Nelson, I thought. The barking has to mean it's Lauren inside. My lungs jumped for oxygen. A runaway dog, that tiny, who can't even bark. In that moment, I thought of his big brown eyes and the way he'd turn up toward me and smile as if to thank me after he'd licked the last bits of food from his dinner bowl. That damn tongue that hangs out a little—he'd wiggle it around to get any food off his nose. There's no way he wasn't smiling then. I'd never really acknowledged that little moment until my mind flashed it at me just then. And now he was God knows where with no collar or tags.

"Go ahead, Richard," Casino prodded with his hand on my shoulder, ushering me forward. We were going to have to face this, one way or another.

I opened the door, and the stench, which I'd forgotten, hit me like a Volvo in a crash test. I got lightheaded. Lauren jumped wildly against my leg. I reached for the light switch and prepared myself to see a room with just Lauren, half dog-empty.

With the burst of light from the chandelier, Casino laughed. It was Nelson that was jumping against my leg. Lauren was sitting on Irene's chair wagging her tail.

"You didn't let me finish," Casino chuckled. "The one on the chair got away from me on the walk, but I got her back. When I saw you panicking, I thought I'd fuck with you a little bit."

He was getting quite a kick out of himself.

"Damn, it smells in here," he said.

"Holy fuck, Casino, I would kick you in the balls if I thought they were big enough to feel any pain," I said.

"Yeah, it was crazy," he went on. "We were heading up the street, and the one took off, got up to Romaine, and then took a right toward Fairfax."

"Holy shit."

"For sure. A couple of people up the street saw me running and screaming and took off after her too," he said. "Nobody could catch her. She was like Barry Sanders out there."

I picked up Nelson. This was the first time I'd held him—and without the gloves on.

"Shut up, Lauren! Shut the fuck up!" I yelled. Her barking was making me want to kill her. *This is twice that she's run. I fucking hate her.*

"She didn't hit Fairfax, did she?" I asked.

"Yeah! She ran right across, no hesitation, near Lola's," he said. This part was no joke to him. "I couldn't believe she didn't get hit. I ran out into traffic myself. I was waving at cars to stop. I'm lucky I didn't get killed."

"Except that I might kill you right now." *You're hardly a hero here,* I thought. *You really screwed up.*

"How'd you get her back?" I asked.

"Luckily, she just froze over there on the other side of the street. I think she freaked herself out and ran out of breath or something," he said. "Then, I was able to grab her and bring her back."

"God, Irene would die if something happened," I said. "And fuck you for fucking with me."

"I couldn't help it," he said. "You're so funny when you're all worked up."

I hate it when people say that to me. People suck. What a shitty night. Thank goodness I was drunk and nothing ended up happening. I have to get a handle on controlling Lauren. And Casino has successfully extricated himself from ever being asked this favor again. Congratulations.

"I've saved that one twice now from running away," he noted.

Well done, you evil genius, I thought. Now they're back to being my responsibility alone.

January 20, 12:20 PM

I figured it out. I bought a set of those rope clips yesterday that rock climbers use, carabiners. I clipped the two leashes together at the handles so that if one gets away, it'd be dragged down by the other like Tony Curtis and Sidney Poitier in *The Defiant Ones*. And then, with the carabiner, I hook the leashes to a belt loop on my pants so they can't get away from me in any way. I have to spin around quite a bit during the walks to keep untangled, but I believe it's a stroke of genius.

January 21, 10:20 AM

First off, I ended up not hearing anything from the design placement agency. I don't know what I'm supposed to feel because maybe they will call today, but I doubt it. My positive thinking has run dry. If and when I stop thinking about having hope, the easier it will be to move on to "Why did I even bother?" To move on. Maybe having something else to not think about will push that down the failure-obsession pipeline. Or maybe they will call today. Maybe Roxy will call today. Either of those things could happen. Both of those things could happen. Both of those things could not happen. Maybe someday I'll get paid for maybes. Maybe.

January 22, 10:55 AM

German philosopher Friedrich Nietzsche said, "Anything which is a living body . . . will strive to grow, spread, seize, become predominant—not from any morality or immorality—but because it is living and because life simply is will to power."

Nelson has spread his dominance over the entire kitchen floor and then some. I must extend my will to power and become dominant in that kitchen. This is our Battle of Kursk. I will throw all my tanks and my best soldiers against his, and may fate bring justice to this land.

5:30 PM

I've got it. If we're trying to dissuade Nelson inside, then we need to persuade him outside. I'd already bought a bag of dog treats, potato and duck flavor.

"The dogs go crazy for them," I was reassured at Tailwaggers.

"Potato? When has a dog shown a craving for a potato?"

"It's agriculture. I don't know," the cashier said. "This is why I'm a checker and not a vet."

So, I'll take a pocketful of treats out with me on the walks. I'm going to institute a strict Treats for Pee program: no treats—any time—except outside, immediately after proper evacuation. Nelson bounces up and down like he's on a pogo stick when he hears the treat bag rattling. He must love potatoes. Today is the end of the treats inside though. Now he's got to earn them on the streets. This is a job. They are his paycheck. It'll feel good, raise his self-esteem, get him off welfare. Through a little discipline, he'll learn some self-respect. Maybe once he learns to go outside, he'll start to understand the daily exchanges from other dogs. I'll use his desire for treats to jump-start his instinctual drives.

9:30 PM

Night walk. First trial with Treats for Pee. Lauren got one. Nothing for Nelson. He lined up right next to her when she got her reward. He's confused, even though I've explained everything to him many times. He needs to figure it out.

January 23, 10:20 PM

Day number two of Treats for Pee. Three walks. Nothing. Neither of them. Lauren is trying to control me. Do they sense that something's up?

January 24, 10:20 PM

Day number three on Treats for Pee. Nothing.
    Nothing.

January 25, 4:00 PM

There's so much activity on the sidewalks of this neighborhood every day that I never knew about. There's a man around the corner on Willoughby—we call him the Shadow Boxer. He's out there in front of his apartment with earbuds on, wearing sweatpants and a sleeveless T-shirt, shadow boxing with slow, purposeful, balanced movements, mixed with quick, repeating jabs, ducks, and undercuts, all with diamond-cutter precision. To the dogs, I say, "There's Shadow Boxer, you guys, let's see if we can get him to talk to us today." But he never does. We walk by silently through his fluttering shadow, like being in a car rolling through a car wash.

He looks to be in his fifties, fighting against the loosening tautness of that decade. His head is shaved except for a short mohawk going down the back, and from it hangs a decorative four-inch braid that whips around with his movements. His arms and neck are thick with muscle and are more tattoo than flesh. There's a large one just below his right jaw that says BRIANNA. Someone he loves. We wonder if Brianna has seen it, or even knows about it, if Brianna is any part of his life anymore outside of the backward-reading memory in his mirror every morning, noon, and night. Maybe it's her memory that he's fighting off against the slow breeze. I may never get to find out if we don't talk. When we walk by, we acknowledge one another with a brief nod, and everyone keeps moving through his shadow and pulling along our own.

6:30 PM

I can't do this latex gloves, surgical mask, laying down a spread of newspaper in a single clean patch thing anymore. I either have to clean the entire kitchen floor or give up entirely. I'm afraid of what that apartment is making me vulnerable to: emphysema, asthma, TB, mesothelioma, black lung. I can't face the idea of how much work it would be to get that kitchen floor clean. Nasty. Fuck.

January 26, 3:45 PM

On our afternoon walk today, we discovered someone invaluable—a professional dog walker and trainer named Austen. I struggle like mad with two dogs, but he walked with six, each some different type of breed and size, as if they were one single membrane.

We ran into him about a half a block south of Waring on Edinburgh. Austen is unshaven and wears blue-tinted spectacles. Glasses that round and small must be called spectacles. I've never understood how people can look at the world through a hue. It must make them feel like they can alter reality. I'd like to look at the world through a blindfold.

Austen is tall and gaunt. Seeing his thinness, I realized that I may have lost a few pounds with these daily walks. He's just slightly fleshier than an empty coatrack. He has the individualistically unwashed air of one who is self-employed and dimly rebellious.

His sallow cheeks frame up a warm skeleton smile when he sees us approaching. "You've got Irene's dogs." He's quick to settle his leashed clients, who all sit dutifully as they allow my mutts to sniff around and underneath them ungraciously.

"Everyone knows Irene's dogs, probably by smell," I said.

"It's the hair." Everything he says frolics through the air like a toddler in a bouncy hut. "I see it as my job to get to know all of the dogs in the neighborhood, since I have to teach these guys to deal with everybody."

He stooped down to give the dum-dums each a treat.

"Wait!" I stopped him. "They can't get treats unless they pee first." Then, calming myself, "We've been out here twenty minutes already."

"Ooooh, you're training them? They aren't house trained?"

"They're in-house trained, unfortunately," I said, and then I explained Irene's arm, my predicament, and the Sisyphus-like failure of my Treats for Pee program.

Austen yanked the treats away. The dogs looked as if they'd just watched the ending of *Brian's Song*.

"You're doing the right thing," he said, "but they're stubborn, huh?"

"They refuse to live in accordance with the laws of nature," I said, "and they are above temptation."

"You need to stick with it. Nothing's impossible. You can teach any dog at any age to do anything," he said, now in human-trainer mode. "As long as you keep them thinking about treats all the time but never give them any, unless it's for the behavior that you're teaching."

I appreciated his encouragement, but I doubted he'd ever come across dogs from a world such as theirs. His clients can afford a dog walker.

We chatted for several minutes. He told me about each of the breeds in his pack as they lounged in the shade of a tree along with the dum-dums. And then he pulled forward a large black dog.

"This is Misty. She's a black Lab, and she's all mine. She's eight years old. She was a stray from Hurricane Katrina." Misty was smiling, and her long tongue hung down like a wet carpet on a clothesline.

"I struggle with people's names. Dog breeds will be impossible. I've never been a dog person," I said.

"You are one now. You just don't know it yet," he said. "But Nelson and Lauren know. Look how they look at you."

He simply had no notion of that absurdity.

He then pointed out with deft humor the irony of our discussion about dog treats when he himself was currently managing a bout with bulimia. "I'm going through a breakup. Just dealing with some boyfriend stress and heartache, that's all."

"I get it. I gain weight from the same thing."

"Oh, lucky you."

He handed me his card and said I should call him if I ever need help or advice. He then recommended a good shampoo, which I presumed he meant for the dogs, and told me they have it at Tail-waggers.

I feel good about meeting him, Sheriff. Less alone. I taped Austen's card to the wall above my computer when I got home. His tag line reads: "Dream the Im-paws-ible Dream." We can do this.

January 27, 1:00 PM

I just got a call from someone named Fay. Her voice sounded as old and saggy as the wires between telephone poles. She said she was a friend of Irene's and had just visited her in the convalescent home.

Convalescent home?

Apparently, the doctor at the hospital moved Irene into a home the second day after her fall. She'll be there until they decide she's capable of coming back to living on her own. Fay said that there's an outside chance they may not let her.

May not let her?

"Well, how's she doing?" I asked.

"She's not happy being there," she said.

I'm not happy being here, I thought.

"She's still in a great deal of pain with her arm," the ancient explained, "so she's unable to get up or down, in or out of bed. Her balance is suffering as well. But she really wants to come home. She misses her little doggies."

Why haven't you or anyone else come to check on them then? I argued in my head.

"How are they doing, little Nelson and Lauren?" she asked.

"Well, I've been checking in on them—"

"Oh, that's wonderful," she interrupted. "Irene was hoping that you would because she knew you had a key. Actually," she chuckled, "at first, the idea horrified her because she thinks that you hate her dogs, but I told her that that just couldn't be so, and not to worry."

It could be so. It could so be so. People have just assumed that I'd suddenly take care of these dogs? I was burning, but I couldn't argue with an old lady on the phone for another old lady laid up in a convalescent home who is crying about her dogs.

"I'm really afraid of what too much worrying could do to her now. She doesn't look well," Fay said. "And this place is awful. The other woman in her room talks to herself day and night, going off on anti-Semitic rants and yelling that the Nazis are coming."

"Does she want the Nazis to come?" I joked.

"I think she does, but it's a little hard to tell with the screaming," she said with a controlled laugh. "It's terrible. Irene is even having trouble reading because of it. She's hoping to get moved to another room."

She should be pushing to get home, not to another room, I thought. But I swallowed my anger because there was a warm mix of sympathy, gratitude, patience, and time in Fay's voice that was softening me.

"Well, tell her not to worry. I'm checking in on them, and keeping them fed and everything," I said.

Does Fay know how awful it is in that apartment? I thought. *Maybe that's why she never came by. She's old. She couldn't handle these dogs anyhow.* I wanted to say, "So if I hadn't gone to check on the dogs, then the two of them would just be in there dead right now. It's that simple, right? That's how much she 'loves' the dogs? Total neglect? She wasn't in a coma over there. It's just a broken arm. Other than the bunkmate, it's probably a lot like a vacation for her—lying around all day watching TV, playing bingo, reading books, sipping Cherry 7UP through a bendy straw, and eating egg sandwiches. And no one comes to check in on the precious dogs? You just assumed I'd be doing this?" But I kept it all in.

Really, Sheriff, what would she have done for me in any kind of reverse situation? She ignored me all this time. And yet she assumes that I would do what I'm doing now?

"Do you know that the dogs aren't trained?" I asked in a desperate lunge toward martyrdom or, in the very least, empathy.

"Oh, I know. I'm sorry," she said. "I've been over there. I know it's bad."

"Well—is she in much pain?" I asked.

"Yes, unfortunately. The place where her arm broke is very high up near her shoulder, so the cast that they have her in puts her in an awkward position. It's hurting her neck and hurting her back. They have her on a lot of pain medication, so she's sleeping a lot and really groggy."

Why don't they sedate the Nazi woman, too? I thought.

"She's not very happy," she explained. "She says the doctor never comes around, and when he does, he doesn't really say anything."

"Does anyone have any idea how long this will be?" I asked.

"Well, my daughter's a nurse, and she said that a broken bone is normally about six weeks to heal, but Irene's a little older, so they can't tell. Plus, as I said, if she can't get some strength back enough to be able to move herself around, I just don't know," Fay explained. "Maybe if they start giving her some physical therapy when the bone mends, it can help."

Her bones must be like eggshells. This could go on forever, I thought. *These dogs need to be put in a kennel.*

And with the clairvoyance that comes with age, Fay continued, "Irene doesn't want to have to put the dogs in a kennel. She's terrified. They're so small and dependent. Plus, it would cost something like sixty dollars a day per dog, and she can't afford that on Social Security. She'd lose them."

Attention all passengers: the guilt trip has reached its destination.

She deserves to lose them, I thought. I couldn't help myself. I have so much anger about this that I couldn't express to Fay. And now guilt? Maybe Irene's in a situation where she can no longer own dogs. That's life. *She couldn't even take care of them properly before this!* And now—*why me?*

At this point, what was I supposed to say, Sheriff? What was I supposed to do? Even if I knew friends or a family somewhere that could house two dogs for a while, I couldn't foist these two—untrained—on anyone. These two that can barely take a normal walk outside.

I'm totally defeated. I was already done with this whole escapade before this call. Now it could be weeks. Treats for Pee isn't working. I can't do it. But those two dum-dums are sitting over there in the kitchen right now, sleeping or just staring off into space.

"Tell her everything will be fine," I said. "The dogs are being fed and walked, and they're fine."

"She'll be so relieved to hear that. I'm sorry I wasn't able to contact you earlier, Richard, but this was the first chance I had to get over here myself, and it doesn't seem like Irene has any other visitors."

"Well, thanks for the call, Fay," I said. And that was it. That was it. I've really stepped in it, Sheriff—with Ralphs bags over my shoes.

3:00 PM

I still haven't heard anything from Roxy. Man, oh man, would she be a big help in this situation. So caring with animals—very, very loving. I don't have that in me. I might be OK trying to teach them to go outside with some encouragement or discipline, but I could never be the way she is. She'd make it seem so easy, make it fun. Damn, and what a fantasy challenge Irene's apartment would be for a cleaner-scrubber girl like her. I think she'd actually be sexually turned on by it. Not kidding. She loves doing laundry and stuff like that. I think it touches a place of maternity inside her. I suppose she's thinking about kids now. She might be a bit OCD with the way that she liked things so clean, but, even so, I only see that as a plus. Who am I kidding? I see everything as a plus. Now I miss her more. But now I'm cleaning up dog shit every day. Not attractive.

6:20 PM

Standing in Irene's kitchen today, watching the dogs eat (yes, Lauren was actually eating), a theory of quantum physics from high school suddenly hit me like a pop quiz. You know we're all . . . well, everything is made up of particles. We as humans, it starts with DNA, then RNA, then cells—all particles. And quantum physics says that the particles themselves are not moving, they're only reacting to fields around them. I just got back to my place and looked it up. Einstein said, "The field is the sole governing agency of the particle." What he means is that the particle is affected by its surroundings, its environment, things that have energy that act upon it, not vice versa. Basically, we can physically see a magnet, but we can't see the magnetic field around it. But when something else is introduced into that magnetic field, that is then what makes the magnets move. I think that's essentially it.

I was so excited to remember this. Mr. Kochinski would be amazed that I retained anything from his class.

There are so many wackos out there, such as Ally, who think that we're all governed by "the universe." Some people think there are spirits around us, and that we have a spirit that affects other people or even draws certain people to us—remember the Law of Attraction? It's our "field."

Well, standing in Irene's kitchen—that universe, that field—I realized that the field has a profound effect on me; that's for sure. Maybe it has the same effect on Irene, or even on the dogs. How can it not? When you walk into a restaurant, the size of it, the lighting, the aromas of the food, the decor, even the amount of people and types of people who are there all have an immediate effect on your desire to stay, your appetite, and your feeling after you've left. This is the same idea. Yes, she, they, created that mess, but maybe it snowballed on itself, tossing over and over to the point where the environment—her field—controls her as a human being. It's physics. I'm thinking, if we can improve and control the field around the dogs, maybe we can improve their habits. I know they're dogs and not humans, but they're made up of particles just the same, and undoubtedly they react differently to various environments they may be in, i.e., a dog in a cage is different from a dog in the front seat of a car.

Ha—you know, Roxy would make all this fun. Plus, she had her way of always putting things "out into the universe," and here I have to make it scientific and mathematical. But we're not thinking about Roxy right now.

What I'm realizing is that to survive this, I'm going to have to clean Irene's kitchen, and I'm going to have to get the dogs to learn to go outside. I guess I'll have to get the dogs clean, too. There's no getting around it. I can't just maintain this mess and hand it off. I've been "just maintaining" the mess of my life, and that's why I'm alone. I guess that's what I was doing when I very first started this log—trying to solve a problem in my "field." Now that problem has been swallowing me whole. I can't let it. I have to rescue myself, or I'm going to end up sedated, lying in a bed in the room with Irene and the Nazi.

That's it. My mind is made up. I'm taking control of this. It's the only way that I can feel in control, right?

11:00 PM

How much do you believe of what I wrote just before? Do you think it's all bullshit? Are people products of their environment, or are the environments products of the people? Is my "fields" theory simply saying that people control their own fate, that life's about choices and control of the will? It seems like an oversimplification, but when I stand in Irene's apartment, it's undeniable that something is evident of something. I just don't know which. Are people victims of their environment or victims of themselves? Which is the extension of which?

Do you believe I can change Irene's apartment and Nelson and Lauren? And what about when Irene comes home?

I haven't even started to do anything over there yet. Do you think I'm looking forward to scrubbing that floor? I've barely been able to tolerate cleaning it in square inches. I'm lying in bed thinking about it instead of sleeping.

Nietzsche said something about life being suffering, and surviving is about finding meaning in that suffering. But he also said that hope prolongs the torments of man. You know, I've always invested too much in hope and come up tormented.

January 28, 9:10 AM

So, Nietzsche himself tormented me in a dream last night: I saw him and Roxy out on a date. So—jealousy. Boom. Anyone smarter. Anyone slimmer. Anyone handsome enough. Anyone at all successful, as in, has a decent job that might interest her for conversation and offer stability, even Friedrich Nietzsche—an overopinionated,

German agnostic philosopher from the 1800s with a mustache the size of a calico cat. Anyone who can make her laugh, or feel safe, or good about herself. Who next, nightmares? Constantine? Alexander the Great? Alexander Graham Bell? Dean Martin? Fred Astaire? A caveman with a buffalo carcass? How about you, real world? Anyone but me. Nietzsche's dead though, so fuck him, his chances are the same as mine. And fuck him being in my dream. Fuck the meaning of dreams. Super-fuck writing them down. Fuck sleep.

9:30 AM

Fuck this entire thing. I'm going in to clean the whole rest of the kitchen floor. I'd love to get this all done in one shot. Like De Niro in *The Deer Hunter*: "One shot is what it's all about. A deer's gotta be taken with one shot."

12:15 PM

Holy God, it was awful—I just took the longest, hottest shower of my life. I only got about a third of the way finished around the path that I'd already cleaned. It's so encrusted that I have to wet and wipe away top layers with 409 and paper towels, then scrub the bottom layer with a brush, then 409 and paper towel that away, and then clean the scrub brush in the sink for the next round. It's all hands-and-knees work. I can only hold my head up so high to keep it away from the rising fumes of blended waste and cleanser. When I think of the soles of Irene's shoes, and the bottoms of those dogs' feet . . . I had to take breaks every five minutes or so.

I was ill prepared. I need a hazmat suit and that industrial spray that NASA used to use to clean off the astronauts when they returned from space. I need so many things. I ran out of paper towels in no time, and 409 is kids' stuff against that floor. The bristles on the brush were leaping off like rats from the *Lusitania*. I need better equipment. I don't have any spending cash, but a trip to the hardware store is a necessity. "One shot." Right. I underestimated the monster-deer.

I underestimated the sensitivity of the alarms in my immune system. I underestimated my intolerance for suffering vs. my ambition.

I laid down newspapers. I'm sure Nelson will take care of those. We're also almost halfway out of the newspapers.

4:00 PM
Back from Tashman's Hardware on Santa Monica. I managed to keep it under thirty dollars. Got a thicker filter mask, kneepads, paper towels, a more robust scrubbing brush, and the strongest cleanser they had. I asked them what they would have recommended for Chernobyl. These are the tools of change. I'm going to get it done.

January 29, 10:20 AM

Took the dogs for a very long walk this morning. We went up Hayworth to Santa Monica then back down the other side of the block all the way to Waring, then west to Edinburgh, back up Edinburgh, then west again down Willoughby all the way to Crescent Heights, and then back again. Neither one of them peed. We went by six or seven sets of people walking their dogs. I stopped each time, trying to socialize these two. (I'm leaving the rubber gloves at home now.)

People chat with me, and I find it pleasant, even though I hate being up this early. These dog owners have their acts together. They all automatically think we have something in common because we have dogs. I don't "have" dogs.

There's a middle-aged French woman named Elise who adores these two. She owns a tired- and sad-looking pug named Omar. When she stops, Omar sits on his rear haunches and pants as if he's just ended his first day of Moroccan desert training with the French Foreign Legion. His mouth is wider than his head. When his jaws are relaxed, he looks like a furry blowfish. His exhaustion makes him calm around the dum-dums.

C'mon, Omar, teach these guys how to behave.

Elise proudly tells me that she drinks a full bottle of wine every day.

"I find your accent to be just as intoxicating."

She smiles. "It is good for you, for your health," she promises in her soft minuet voice, "and for your happiness. It gives freedom to the mind."

I concur.

She's not looking too bad for a dedicated alcoholic. Whenever she sees us, she crouches down to pet the dogs. I cringe inside when people do this. I don't know where my responsibility lies in telling people that the dogs are so polluted that the EPA should categorize them as walking hot zones. Elise must be able to tell, unless some of that daily bottle is getting tipped in place of coffee, too. Maybe animal lovers just don't care, or maybe French people just don't care. I always remind her that they're not mine, they are Irene's, so as to disembarrass myself.

I try to do my best to disguise my distress. Sometimes the other dogs are friendly like Omar, and sometimes they go crazy. Nelson and Lauren usually jump around for several seconds before they decide if they're going to get close or not. I'm trying to get them to smell other dogs to find a scent that they can get interested in and want to check out every day. That's what Austen told me dogs do.

12:45 PM

I wonder if their olfactory receptors are so damaged by their own foul existence that they can no longer pull those other dogs' scents up into their brains. I feel that way myself after spending time over there. I can't smell my antiperspirant after I put it on anymore. Loss of smell is a sign of Alzheimer's. What if I can't tell if I'm smelling bad? There's no way that Irene has any concept of how she smells. We all have moments of not caring, but it's a whole other level to live beyond its self-detection. No wonder Lauren has no regular appetite. She has no interest in food because she can't taste it. Then she gorges when she's starving. That's probably why she's overweight.

I couldn't take any more time walking. We'd been out there for forty-five minutes. I'm so frustrated that they didn't go. I guess I'll have to keep taking them out all day, because I don't want them to do it inside while I'm there. I lose it when they do it right in front of me.

January 30, 5:25 PM

It's done. The floor is back to being a floor. It's so clean you could, well, walk on it. Took all day with so many breaks outside. Walked the dogs a few times, but they'd been going on the living room rug. That rag has got to go, too. I get so angry when I see that they peed. They used to just scatter when I got angry, but now that they've gotten used to me, they stay in place and hunch up, and cower, and give me the sad orphan eyes. Lauren trembles like a puddle in a thunderstorm. It's as if they know guilt, but I know they don't. They've lived lives of pure guilt-free indulgence. But when they stay still and listen to me, I feel respected. Now I want them to develop self-respect, respect for their space and belongings. I gave them a speech titled "Why We Walk." I've given them a clean kitchen floor. It's a new lease on fresh-scented living. They have to take it.

Just in case, I covered the entire floor with newspaper. It's like a disposable floor.

11:30 PM

Maybe I'm high from the cleanser fumes—or maybe because I got a text from Roxy tonight saying hi, and that she thinks about me. We went back and forth a little, but I wasn't saying much. I want her to say things at this point—not me. She said she'd like to see me. Part of me is ecstatic, but part of me is still spilling blood. Don't know what to do. I'm excited though.

Got very good news today. That anesthesia client's "new ideas" work that went away shortly after the watch store has come back, some of it. That should give me some stability, if it stays, and if I can stretch everything out. Amazing how quickly things go and come.

Took the dogs for a late walk. Lauren peed. She does that once in a while now. Got her treat. Poor Nelson—nothing.

January 31, 11:00 AM

No updates on Irene. I have Fay's number in my phone now, so I could call, but I don't feel like it. I don't want to have to answer a lot of questions, and I don't want Fay coming over here and finding out that I've been cleaning and then inflame Irene's mental malaise. She might freak just that I touched her newspapers. Who knows?

I wonder how Fay feels, being old herself, when she visits Irene in the convalescent home. It's got to be frightening. As lonely as I am now, I fear those days more than anything, and the thought of being alone in my life at that time, the way my father was, makes me want to swallow a bottle of death vitamins right now. I think that's what I'd do if it comes to that. I certainly don't want to end up like Irene.

Irene was a lawyer. Says she lived in Beverly Hills. I don't know why she has absolutely nothing now, but, at this point in my life, I'm way behind where she was. I have debt, no savings, no 401k or retirement plan. I could end up entirely dependent on the government. Euthanasia comes from Greek, meaning "happy death." There should be a word for "happy suicide" because I think sometimes people do it to be happier.

2:45 PM

Today a neighbor from a few doors up the street shouted out to me, "Hey, how's that old lady doing? I don't see her out here anymore, and I see you with the dogs."

The level of concern on his face surprises me, being that he doesn't know Irene's name.

"Is she all right?" It's Nathan. His voice is like rubbing two chalkboards together. Nathan is frail. He had a very rough go of it as a youngster, and ever since, really. He's survived Hodgkin's lymphoma. That battle left his heart weak, and he's had two heart attacks without having yet turned thirty-five. He's a very pleasant human being, not a touch of bitterness shows, but he keeps death very near in his thoughts, perhaps so as never to be surprised. He is the sweetest specter of the beyond that one could possibly have as a neighbor.

He talks very openly about his poor health. That's probably why he wants to know about Irene. In fact, everyone I meet on these walks leads with their current and/or chronic pains or diseases. I know people better by their health records than by their names.

Nathan's hair is long but very thin, the strands tied desperately into a ponytail. He wears a wiry goatee, and thick glasses sit at an angle atop the rugged terrain of what could be a former boxer's nose, or the nose of someone who got beat up a lot as a kid. He's freckly and sun-sensitive, as he shades his face with his hand, unfortunately leaving his hand vulnerable to more freckling.

"I don't really know how she is, but she's fine" is how I usually begin my response to that question to everyone, and then I explain that her arm is broken, etc.

"So, you're taking care of the dogs?"

I wondered at the suspicion in his tone. Does this look like some master scheme to take Irene for all her mismatched Tupperware?

"What if she doesn't come back?" he asked, as if I'd thought about any of this beyond each present, agonizing moment.

"She'll be fine. Her friend is visiting her," I reassured him.

"Old people just die. Accidents like this take them down," he said. "They fall, then they get an infection, staph or something, and they croak," he unassured me.

Of course, he wasn't wrong. My mother died of a deep vein thrombosis after a two-night hospital stay for some chest congestion, just a clot that had loosened from within her leg and shot up to her lung because her legs hadn't been moved enough while she lay there in bed. And I told you about Roxy's dad.

"I'm positive that nothing bad will happen to her, and she'll be home soon." That felt like lies.

"These dogs are going to be yours someday," he said with a sinister, sandpaper laugh.

That felt like . . . Nope. Nope. Nope.

February

February 1, 9:00 PM

Roxy called, left me a message that she wants to see me, that we should talk. God, I don't want to get broken up with all over again. But I need to see her. I called her back. We set something up for Wednesday here. It gives me a reason to straighten up.

February 2, 1:00 PM

One of the big problems that mucks up these dogs is all that hair. It's so long under their bodies that it drags along the floor. Plus, hair grows out of their faces, keeps growing and growing. Now that the floor is clean, I want to get them clean too. Might be bath time.

Started straightening up my own place, too.

February 3, 10:20 AM

I guess it was true about those hospice visits. Fay called this morning to give me an update. Nothing's changed. Irene sees the doctor once a week, and he appears and says, "You're doing fine. It'll be a little while," and then leaves. The Nazi in her room still doesn't like Jews. She's been trying to sneak out at night, apparently setting off some kind of hidden mattress alarm again and again every time she gets out of bed.

Fay explained to me how she and Irene met. Fay's husband had been diagnosed with stage four lung cancer and was in hospice. At the time, Fay still worked as a floor supervisor at Macy's, and she could only be home in the evenings. "It was an awful time," she explained.

One day as she arrived in her husband's room, Irene was there at his bedside holding his hand, talking with him, and they were laughing.

"I hadn't seen Henry laugh in quite a while," she said.

It turned out that Irene had been visiting him every afternoon as a hospice volunteer.

"It just meant the world to me to find that out," Fay said. "And Irene being such a kind and intelligent person, it felt as if an angel had been given to us." She said it relieved her of some of the guilt that she couldn't leave work on so many days. "That's always one of the most difficult parts of this for families, but when you experience it yourself, that you can't control your schedule in such a hard time, it's terrible."

Fay said she's forever grateful for what Irene did for her Henry.

So all the while that Sophie was barking when Irene wasn't home, and I was sitting here writing this log, she might have been at Henry's bedside. Or someone like Fay's Henry.

February 4, 11:45 PM

I'm nervous about Roxy coming over tomorrow. I don't know what to think. I am weakness.

February 5, 9:10 PM

Roxy was here. When I opened the door, she stood stiff as a Secret Service agent. She smiled and said hello, but it had all the warmth of a stack of cinder blocks.

We're already broken up, I thought. *This can't go anywhere but up. Think, or at least act, positive, you idiot. Wait,* I countered to myself, *what if this is the establishment of the friend zone?* Confidence gone.

She wore a white cotton top and a long, light brown cotton skirt, more like a stiff burlap, that refused to define her hips. I miss them. She could have just stepped off of a Conestoga wagon. She'd pinned her hair back very tightly, along with every fiber of her sex appeal. If she could have, I think she would've left her long legs entirely in the car before coming in.

Before even a word was spoken, I already couldn't reach my sinking heart. Nietzsche said that for a man to just be friends with a woman he must be "assisted by a little physical apathy." She was, consciously or not, trying to give that apathy a forceful push. But I didn't care about the *Little House on the Prairie* outfit—turns out my heart had only sunk as low as my pants. Her beauty eviscerates me. The only eyes I ever want to see. I trembled like Lauren during a scolding. Roxy's rejection of me was, in part, a scolding for not having my shit together. *It still isn't together.* Fear mixed with attraction in a gust of adrenaline. The achievement of her love was all that mattered again. Her loving me gave me existence. She's here, so I exist.

She must have missed me. Why would she have texted me and be standing in my living room right now? Is this just an inspection? If it is, then she has thoughts about coming back. She needs to see how I'm doing, how she feels around me. My apartment shone like a model home. She used to love it here when she called it cozy—before it became too small and pathetic.

No hug as she came in. She set down her purse and sat on the sofa. *The things we'd done on that sofa.* I sat here at my desk chair. It was too chilly on the couch.

We chitchatted. I hate that word, but that's what we did. All headlines, no stories. Work was good. I told her mine was good.

(I'd picked up that big web project.) Her family was good. I told her mine was good. She'd just gotten her hair trimmed. I told her I'd recently gotten mine trimmed as well. All I wanted to talk about was *us*. This was us both talking about *I*, and in scant, distancing detail—until, that is, I mentioned the dogs.

It was as if I'd told her I'd just invented ice cream. Her posture lifted, her head notched slightly to the left, and the hard scowl was yanked up by strings of curiosity: "How'd it happen? How is Irene? What are those dogs like?"

When I got talking about Irene's apartment, Roxy's inner Nancy Drew kicked in. She had to see everything for herself.

"Can we go over there?" she asked.

Yep, she wants to make this fun. I love her, I thought. "The air isn't quite clean in there yet. You might need a mask and gloves."

She jumped to her feet. "Oh my God! Give them to me, and let's get over there!"

Everything about her had suddenly changed into a kid about to explore a cave. All she needed was a flashlight and popcorn to leave a trail.

It's turned into us, I thought, as I handed her a mask from the pack. "I hope you're ready."

When we got inside, her head spun around like an owl's. "Oh my God," she said, muffled by the mask.

Even though I'd cleaned the kitchen, the air still metered on this side of rancid. The dogs ran to me, Lauren barking away, but I dismissed them and went to the kitchen to wrap up the dirty newspapers.

"The dogs like you," she said with surprise as she pulled at a window to open it. But the window was stuck. I gave her a hand. "They really do." Her eyes were smiling brightly above the rim of the mask, her eyelashes like petals of midnight hyacinth.

"They'd better. We've been through a lot, the three of us."

"Oh my God—look," she said, and she darted to a bookcase. She pulled a thick binder from a shelf. *"Ethics School Workbook—State Bar of California, 1970.* She really was a lawyer. Look at all these books."

"It's mostly classics—"

"But these are all law books—*Law and the Family, California Proof of Injury*. And here, these—*The Decorative Arts* and *Decorating with Flowers*." She opened one. "*The Art and Architecture of China*. Oh, her house must have been gorgeous."

"I thought these vases might've been Chinese," I said. I was enthralled in her excitement.

"Look at this," and she handed me a heavy coffee table book. We both held it. "*Art Deco Graphics*." We looked at each other. Neither one of us said *IT*—we just smiled and began turning the pages.

Lauren pawed at Roxy's leg. She stooped down to pet the two of them with a sympathetic, "Awwww."

They already like her better than me.

"Oh, their hair is all caught up in their mouths. This is awful."

"I know," I said. "I'm planning to give them baths soon. I bought some shampoo here, but I wanted to get the floors cleaned first, so—"

She stopped me. "I have to cut this hair off. They can barely see, and they're going to choke themselves to death. Are there scissors in here?"

She was on my team. There were scissors in the kitchen drawer. "Here you go," I said.

She had carte blanche. She knew more about dogs than I did. "If they're going to choke to death, it's going to be me that does it to them, not their own hair," I sort of joked.

She put them on the newspaper and began chopping hair away. They were incredibly well behaved in her hands. She cut all the long hair from the sides of their mouths, about six inches in length, and everything above their eyes and around their ears. You could see the relief on their faces. She even cut a lot of the body hair that had hung to the floor. They looked good, younger, zippier immediately.

"Wow, they have faces," I said. "Their eyes are as big as pancakes." I was so happy to be with her I was going to bust. I thought about the engagement ring.

"We need to give them a bath," she said.

We—yes, "we." And we did. They're so small, they both fit into the sink at once. The first rinse released a toxic cloud of biological decay, but we were laughing like hell at these two tiny dogs, soaking wet and all nervous. I held them as she washed them.

The woman you love, giving these desperate dogs a bath, speaking in those soothing tones to keep them calm, laughing at their sweet vulnerability—is there anything more wonderful, Sheriff?

Her hands slid slowly through the soapy water and hair, scratching gently into their scalps and backs and bellies. I could feel it myself, how she used to rub my neck and tug at my hair when we kissed.

"Nelson, Nelson!" she'd say as she'd put her nose to his, and he'd smile through his soaking hair, his tongue lapping at the water pouring over his head.

Our hips were touching as we leaned against the sink, our arms and hands working together. We were laughing at every move the dogs made. *We're a team.* When we finished the bath, we tied them up outside to let them air dry as we brushed them in the late afternoon sun. Roxy braided the long hair on their heads. They looked very hip. We didn't talk about much, except about the dogs, training them, etc., and the beauty and the warmth of the sunshine. Three happier dogs you've never seen, Sheriff: Nelson, Lauren, and me.

We took them for a short walk. She chose Nelson. It was then that she told me she was now "dating." She didn't say whom, and I didn't ask. There wouldn't be any answer that I could take hearing. She said she was happy. It wasn't convincing enough for me to believe, but it was convincing enough to hurt. The happiness heroin drained away; the shakes growled back. But I had to act happy. It's the only socially acceptable reaction in this situation.

"I'm going to get out there soon myself," I said, half wanting her to know that I'd truly been waiting for her, and half wanting her to feel a pang about the idea of my seeing someone new. Neither seemed of any use.

And she left. She kissed me on the lips and said, "I'm glad you're doing well." Those aren't even friendship words—that's complete separation.

I don't know what happened today. Can you tell me?

The apartment looks lonelier when it's clean.

February 9, 1:00 PM

Sorry. Lost weekend. Tough couple days.

Been walking the dogs though.

I'll get back on board.

February 10, 10:00 AM

Got a call from Fay. Not much change. When Irene was awake, she asked about the dogs. I told Fay I'd given them a bath. She got all excited and asked if she could come by to take them over for a visit. "Irene has two little doggy carry bags somewhere under her bed, I think they are. I think I can handle them if they're in those little bags," she said.

The phrase "somewhere under her bed" made me shudder. *What can I do to avoid going under her bed?* I thought.

"Do they allow animals?" I asked.

"Oh yes, uh-huh. I saw the cutest little beagle in here on Monday, and I thought of Nelson and Lauren, but I didn't say anything to Irene because I thought her dogs'd be too dirty," she said, "but now that they're bathed, it'll be fine."

I had no choice. Maybe seeing the dogs looking clean and groomed and happier will help motivate Irene to heal more purposefully.

1:15 PM

Seeing Austen on our walks has been a big help. He says that there's some product at the pet store that can help not just eliminate the odors but also de-mark where the dogs have gone so that they don't go in that same spot again. He also says that I may have to put Nelson in a crate to keep him from going inside.

"Dogs will not go in their own confined space," he proclaimed. He said he has a small crate he could loan me.

I don't know. Putting a dog in a tiny box, I just don't know. I'd be leaving him in there overnight with no one around. I just don't know. Irene would freak out if she found out.

4:00 PM

I found that odor eliminator product at Tailwaggers. It's called Organic Marvel. It says that it's "guaranteed to eliminate pet musk from unplanned urination incidents or your money back." Get this: "Dissuades spot resoiling." Sounds like dog counseling.

Do you think it'll work? I don't know if it's ever gone up against anything the likes of Nelson. He's undissuadable. We'll see.

8:20 PM

OK, sprayed the Organic Marvel. Had to leave no newspaper down in that area to see if it works. If neither of them hits that area, then it's a winner. I should be able to expand that area until I eliminate their desire for any spotting in the kitchen.

February 11, 2:50 AM

I found some tequila in my cupboard, or it found me, gave me a couple hours. My family went to a bullfight once in Tijuana when I was seven on a sideline trip during a vacation to Disneyland. It was a horror show—no glory in it, no sport, no fine art—just bloody abuse and terror. When I began this log to you, Sheriff, I might have described myself as the tormented bull, poked and jabbed by the lances of the picadors as Sophie barked away—before the kill. Maybe I'm the clown. No, that's rodeos where there are clowns. I'm not doing anything to change anything. Like being seven years old and being unable to stop a bullfight. Maybe I can. Get in the ring.

11:15 AM

I'm going to have to increase the frequency of the walks. I'll have to get there very early in the morning, not 10:00 AM anymore. Set an alarm for 7:00 and rush over there before they go on the newspaper. They've become immune to the chemical suggestion of the Organic Marvel. I knew those poor enzymes never stood a chance—the Maginot Line of guarantees. I'm going to write them a letter. They need to go back to the lab and bring in some more

challenging test dogs. So I'm still cleaning up after them every day.
I hate getting up early, but I hate cleaning up after them, especially
to start the day.

If I can get the dogs trained by the time Irene gets home, then her
place can stay clean. I don't care if she's miserable or depressed. If she
comes home to a clean apartment and happy, trained dogs, her spirits
will recoup what her "field" had destroyed. Tomorrow, we begin.

February 12, 11:10 AM

Alarm went off at 7:00. Just couldn't do it. Up too late last night
watching *Papillon* on Turner Classic Movies. Steve McQueen is awesome. There's a man's man. Papillon tried to escape from a prison
on Devil's Island a bunch of times before finally getting to freedom.
I found it inspiring, but it didn't end until 3:00. I dreamed that I had
a tattoo of a Yorkshire terrier on my chest.

Has anyone ever tried to escape on you? Run? Seems there's no
way to recapture someone without shooting at them or swinging the
baton. Ever used it? When I think of you whaling away on someone's
hamstrings, I don't like it. I've never met anyone who could do that.
See, I know soldiers, but they fight the enemy. You're dealing with
citizens. I know you guys have to protect yourselves. You either
shoot someone if it's life or death, or subdue and arrest them. I don't
understand the beating and beating someone just about to death part.

I don't think I could beat someone, even if I were exploding.
Remember that car wreck I mentioned when I was seventeen? Still
have scars on my face, neck, and chest from it. I've felt enough pain
to not want to throw it on someone else. I'd be a terrible partner
out there, wouldn't I. Maybe if I had the right training. I can't even
get myself up at 7:00 AM. I'm going to do it tomorrow. I certainly
didn't like having to clean up this morning, and then the dogs did
nothing outside. I'm through with that.

February 13, 8:00 AM

The crack of dawn mission isn't working. Can't get there early
enough before they pee inside. If we were on a farm, the rooster

would be woken up each day by the tiny tinkling sprinkling sound of Nelson peeing. His name should be Sunrise.

I told them, "Today we're going for a real walk—westward—and we're not going to stop until you both pee. I swear we're going to go past Crescent Heights, past La Cienega if we have to. I'll walk you two through to Beverly Hills, and if that's not far enough, then we'll go to Westwood, then West L.A., and, if we get all the way to the Santa Monica Pier without peeing, then the three of us walk into the ocean and we end this whole thing."

6:25 PM

I've finally given in to the crate. Austen lent me his. I've no other choice. It's going to be awful. Tonight, after the midnight walk. Hopefully, Nelson'll take to it and just rock himself to sleep. If he starts going nuts in there, I don't know what I'm going to do. Austen says he'll settle into it. I've had plenty of guarantees though. Cleaning him up after an accident in that plastic shoebox would be a nightmare—way worse than picking up newspapers.

Austen said, "I love their hair all trimmed and with the braids—how clean they are." Everyone we see mentions it.

11:20 PM

Did it. Man, oh man, it was painful. The crate. I put one of my kitchen chair cushions in the crate to make it soft for him. He did not want to go in. I spoke in the sweetest voice I had—I pretended to be Roxy. I had to put some treats in there to get him inside. The first break in the Treats for Pee program. He got me. It was 11:00 at night already. His eyes kept asking, "Why? Why?"—as if he didn't know.

Lauren was panting with anxiety. I probably was, too. I'd transferred Nelson into solitary. There's no way that this doesn't feel like a punishment. Now he is Papillon. As caged as I felt with Sophie's barking, there's Nelson the Mute, unable to speak, and now unable to roam. He looked at me with the innocence of a newborn. And when the grated metal door closed, he put his nose up against it as if the air inside were poisoned. I tapped his nose.

"Goodnight, Nelson, it's going to be OK, my friend. I'll be here at sunup. You know I'll come back. I always do," I told him. I don't know if he believed me.

February 14, 6:40 AM

Morning one in the crate. I didn't sleep well, woke up at 4:00 thinking about little Papillon over there in solitary. In the movie, Papillon would pace back and forth in his cell. He measured five steps across, and would quietly count one through five as he shuffled wall to wall, hour upon hour, to keep his body alive. When they released him, he stepped out into the corridor and slowly counted his first few steps of freedom. When he got to number six, he collapsed. I don't think that Nelson can count, but I'll understand if he collapses with his first burst of freedom on this morning's walk.

The sky offered only a bare hint that another day might be coming. It'd been a chilly night, and I wondered if the dogs'd missed the warmth of each other's bodies the way that I miss Roxy's. When I got inside, Nelson was flipping out in the crate as if there were a cockfight going on in there.

I didn't know what I'd find. I made him wait while I leashed up Lauren, then knelt down and opened his little cell door. He tried to jump onto my lap but slipped to the floor. I was his jailer, yet, at this moment, he loved me more than anything. Has that ever happened to you, Sheriff? If you've ever wondered what Stockholm syndrome is, this was it. He jumped and jumped like a paranoiac's electrocardiogram.

"Don't do anything yet," I warned Nelson's lower digestive tract. I hurried to get the leashes on and hustle them outside. I glanced inside the crate—nothing. Good. We rushed outside—and it worked. It worked! Right away it worked, in fact. Solitary confinement, life inside the crate, gave Nelson a sense of ownership over his territory, an understanding that he wanted an area around himself clean—a field. As bad as I felt last night locking him in there, I was now exuberant to give him his first earned Treats for Pee reward. He snapped and snapped at it, jerking his head from side to side, proudly emphasizing each bite, all the while looking up at me as if to say, *I knew I could do it. I'm a grown-up. I'm part of the team.*

It was a great walk after that. The pressure was off. Now we could stride along the sidewalks simply as a way to get a bit of exercise and fresh air to start off the day. We cheerily greeted everyone we met—the super-early dog walkers, the self-disciplined early-riser people with real jobs. The dogs were clean. They looked great, and now they are trained. We graciously accepted many compliments on our improved appearance. When Elise saw us, I wished she'd had some wine in her bag so that we could raise a toast under the trees shading us from the eastern sun around us.

When I got them home, I mussed their hair, teased them, and let their smiling faces fill me with pleasure. But then—a dilemma: *Does Nelson go in the crate during the day now?* Lauren can walk around, but Nelson would have to sit in there and watch her? Doesn't seem right. At nighttime, he'd be sleeping, but during the day, it seems extra cruel. I don't want to traumatize his whole personality away. That's why you use solitary, right, Sheriff? You want to modify a prisoner's behavior, his personality, his psychological makeup, right? Practically lobotomize the man with the blunt force of his own thoughts day and night. But if I don't put him in there, he might not remember how he held it during the hours of darkness.

Truly, the only acceptable outcome of this war is a Carthaginian peace—total subjugation as the Romans did to Carthage. I may only have a couple more weeks to get Nelson in order. I have to convince him that the crate is his home, and that it's OK. The new deal that I struck with myself is that I'd check in over there every couple hours, come hell or high water, and get him out for a walk and maybe some playtime. If he can earn a constant stream of treats outside, then it may mollify the institutional horrors of life behind bars. I guess you guys call that "rec time."

I coaxed Nelson into his crate, and when I closed its door, Lauren went to it and pressed her face against its window. Then she and

Nelson touched noses, as if she were a sad wife, and she plopped herself back onto her mourning pillow. Lauren's got real intelligence, and it's causing her pain. When I see her devotion, I wonder if Roxy misses me, if she ever lies curled up on her bed and thinks about us and what we had. I don't even know if she's in her bed alone anymore. That knifes me. So much I don't know and can't control.

But I can control what's happening here. I'll go back in a couple hours and get the dogs outside again. I have deep faith in this combination of Treats for Pee and the Carthaginian Crating.

I believe in you, Nelson. I do, my boy, I do.

11:50 AM

Fay is coming by today to pick up the dogs and take them to visit Irene. I hid the crate. I don't think Fay would understand because . . . who am I to be crating someone else's dog? I'm positive she'd tell Irene. Then Irene'd get so angry she'd go blind in her other eye. Glad I thought of that. Fay can see the newspapers. Well, she'll see the cleaner apartment for the first time, too. Those home improvements earn me the right to crate Nelson. Not sure she'd see it that way though. She's old. She might not think I have any rights.

2:40 PM

Fay just stopped by to pick up the dogs. She's very old, but upright, wearing ambitious running shoes and a tracksuit. Her hair is dyed GMO-apple red and permed in tight curls to camouflage areas of thinness that shine through like white stucco under ivy. From behind her still-dark transition lenses, she couldn't believe how good the dogs looked, "All clean and soft and with their hair cut so nicely. I'm just thrilled for them." She cradled Lauren in her arms. "Honestly," she said, "driving over here, I was worried about even having to touch the dogs. Now I can't keep my hands off of them."

When she saw the sparkling kitchen, you'd have thought she'd won the Publishers Clearing House. By now I'd cleaned the counters, the shelves, it was all done.

"The floor is white!" she said, with the same exuberance I imagine she'd had when she heard that Lee had surrendered to Grant.

Indeed it is, even whiter than your dentures, I kept myself from saying.

"This is just incredible." Then she stopped herself, her wrinkles dropped toward concern, and the corners of her mouth hit the ground. "I wonder how Irene is going to take this."

"Well, she's going to have to take it," I said. "I cleaned it because I have to be in here every day, and I couldn't take it as it was."

"Irene seems to feel comfortable with her place a mess," she said. "It's a safety net, and if things are changed, she might not react positively."

"Do you want me to make it filthy again for her before she gets back?"

She laughed. "No, and it would take years. I don't know how you did this!"

Her acknowledgment felt good. Only she and Roxy—and you and, I guess, Casino and Austen know I'm doing this. I didn't even know I was "doing this."

"The next step is the dogs," I announced. "I want them to learn to stop going inside so the floors and the air can stay this way."

"Are you Houdini?" Fay joked with her most recent cultural reference.

I thought of the crate. "No, but I do have a few tricks up my sleeve."

She complimented me again on what I had done, and then she left, an eighty-eight-year-old on her way to visit the convalescent home, dogs in tow. I've been lacking compliments lately, Sheriff. I've hardly left the house. Fay is getting around more than I am. The things she said, the astonishment on her old face, were rewarding. I know Roxy thinks it's nice that I'm doing this. She did that day. I never would have done anything like this before, Sheriff. Doesn't that mean something to a woman?

6:30 PM

Fay just returned with the dogs. She was gone for three hours. I was dying to know when Irene would be coming back. *Is she seeing the doctor? How did the Nazi feel about dogs? Does she hate them the way I used to?*

Fay parked in the driveway, and before I carried the dogs into the house, I suggested that it'd be nice if we walked them together, but she felt too tired. Her shoulders had dropped beyond her osteoporosis. *She has bad news*, I thought. At this, I was split with conflict. All I'd wanted for the last two months was for Irene to come home, but now I'm in the middle of a job that's not finished. Nelson isn't even close to being trained, and Lauren isn't fully dependable either. The front room and the bedroom are still a mess, so if Irene comes home early, then all of my effort will have gone for nothing, and these poor dogs will go back to their midcentury-slovenly lifestyle. I need more time. I need at least two more weeks. So, I wanted Irene's doctors to keep her in that home.

I looked down at Nelson who was sitting on his hind legs looking up at me. It feels like he's my dog. I know he's not, but I don't want to give him away. We've been through too much together, and he's happier now.

"Have the dogs said anything?" I asked.

"The dogs?"

"Oh, no—the *doctors*." Wow. "I meant to say the doctors. Have they said anything?"

"Oh, it's still the same routine. They stop in once a week and tell her she's doing fine but that it'll take some time and to just be patient," she said. "Irene is very anxious. She's still not sleeping. Her roommate is awful, and the mattress alarm keeps going off in the middle of the night."

None of us involved in this are sleeping, I thought.

Fay's wrinkle lines were now fully collapsed. There was still something that she had to tell me.

"She must have been elated to see the dogs," I said, trying to lighten her mood, and mine—as some positive words might be nice right now.

"Well, it made her very happy," she said. "Poor Nelson peed right on her bed as soon as I set him down. I felt so awful about that. Irene was thrilled to have them with her though, just so tickled. It was good to see her smiling. They cuddled right up to her. They all miss each other."

"Excellent," I said. *Gross*, I thought.

"But," she continued, "when she got the dogs close, and she noticed their hair had been cut down, she got really upset."

"Upset? Upset about what?"

"She prides herself on the dogs' long hair," she said. "They were both meant to be show dogs, and Yorkshire terrier show dogs always have the long hair. In fact, when Nelson was young, he won several prizes. It wasn't until his hair turned this blondish color that he was excluded from the circuit."

It wasn't because he'd peed all over the arena floor? I fought back in my head.

"You mean to tell me, Fay, that, with this apartment being the mess that it was, and the dogs as matted, smelly, and dirty as they were, when Irene was walking them up and down Hayworth Avenue, she thought she was parading them like show dogs?"

"Pretty much, I suppose, yes," she said in her quiet, humble tone. I sensed sympathy from behind her shaded trifocals, because she knew that this was nuts. "Irene is a very depressed person. She has very little to go on, so if her imagination gives her comfort, I don't want that taken away. She'd even started crying about their hair."

Wait 'til Roxy hears this, I thought. *If we ever talk again—or we could talk tomorrow. I don't know.*

"But it's only trimmed away from their eyes and mouths so that they can see and eat without choking. That hair that sits in their mouths gets so foul."

"I know," she said. "But there's quite a bit taken off their bodies, too. I tried to explain to her that maybe that's what you were trying to do, but she was pretty livid. She's under a lot of stress. She asked me to tell you, or ask you, to please not touch their hair anymore."

When I first got in here, I wouldn't touch them at all, I thought.

"I'm under a lot of stress too, Fay. Does anyone think I'm thrilled to be doing this? Their hair'll grow back."

"She said it'll take four years."

"Good—that'll give her something to live for," I said before I calculated that Fay herself likely has one claw in the crypt, and four years is no laughing matter. But I was angry. I was overreacting to Irene's overreaction. And I'm supposed to be the sane one in this asylum.

But why does everyone just let Irene be crazy? I thought. *If she's so depressed, why let her do all these depressing things?*

Fay sighed and apologized about the upset, which had nothing to do with her, told me that Irene might be out in two weeks if the bone is healing properly, and then she and her jogging shoes shuffled out to her car and were gone.

Both dogs were at my feet, waiting for treats. "You guys are causing me more stress and frustration than anyone I've ever met."

I walked them. The sun was warm. Lauren earned a treat. Nelson didn't. It's tough to give a treat to one dog and not the other. The look of sad confusion that Nelson gives me erodes my resolve like waves over a sandcastle, but I have to stick with the plan. He has to want the potato and duck badly enough to change.

When we got back, I put Nelson in the crate. It took a lot of convincing after such a social afternoon. It's a ritual now that Lauren goes to the door and touches noses with him. I have to stick to my guns.

10:00 PM

It was Valentine's Day today. I hope you and your lovely had a nice date or something together. Should I text Roxy? Roxy. It burns in my belly like a gunshot wound day and night. When I drink, I feel lifted from this earth. Soft, fluid endorphins kick in, and I float with the warm adrenaline and her beautiful sister, dopamine. What do I want to be true? What do I know to be true? What is Roxy thinking? Doing?

I don't know anything, but the negative thoughts are more convincing than anything else. They battle—loss and hope. When I drink, the straitjacket falls loose. I feel like I could be wanted, that I could be attractive. I'm losing weight. My knee is feeling better. I have some work trickling in. I have the goals with the dogs. I hope when Irene comes home the clean place will electroshock her into a more positive approach to living. I'm spending so much time thinking about what these two women might be thinking and how they might behave or react to things that I've framed up a whole architecture of dilemmas for my head.

What am I doing to myself? Why can't I let things go? I care about Roxy, and I care about these dogs now. Hearing Irene's story, I care about her, too. I didn't know how much I cared about Roxy until she was gone, and now I want to be with her for the rest of my life. I didn't care at all about Irene before she broke her arm, and now I want her to have a better life. I hated the dogs, and now I have visions of them staying clean. Nuts.

I'm going to be terribly disappointed if it's a crash trifecta. What then—when I have to go back to my own life in more isolation than I had before? More time in my own head arguing and criticizing. A bottle of red wine will ambush that. I just have to try to keep that spirit alive when the dopamine valves close. Roxy was a supply—laughter, beauty, touch, surprise, joy, intellectual ecstasy. I've crashed. The only laughter I get now is from Nelson with those big eyes and the way that crazy tongue sticks out. He has no idea how dumb he looks. I want to feel the way those dogs feel when they get their treats. I want to wag my tail. I've got myself so closed up and held down waiting for Roxy to come back, to change her mind, that I can't be happy about anything.

February 15, 7:45 AM

I just went back over there, let Nelson out, and took them for a walk. The crate worked again. They both got treats. It's killing me having him in that crate. Just killing me. He can't bark, and I picture him sitting in there trying to, doing that empty chomp with that little snort that comes out his nose. He's probably so unhappy in there. I can't take it.

2:30 PM

I got a text from Roxy just now. Only two words: "Bags! Bags!" It's another one of our little expressions we used to say all the time. Actually, it came from my father. He did all the grocery shopping. He would hit the four local grocery stores on Saturdays hunting down the lowest prices item by item. He had five mouths to feed plus Mom, so it was always a giant trip. Whenever he got home, he'd yell, "Bags! Bags!" in his gruff, gravelly voice to get us off our asses and help grab the rest of the groceries out of the station wagon. So, whenever Roxy or I got home from shopping, we'd text "Bags! Bags!" from the car. It always made us laugh.

She texted me that today. At first I thought it meant she'd just parked right outside of my apartment, actually with bags like some sort of surprise, but I looked and she wasn't there, and there's the awful memory of the Breakup Bags, which I'm sure she wasn't registering.

Was she just carrying grocery bags somewhere and thought of that? Aren't these things off limits once it's over, Sheriff?

I don't know what to think or how to react to it this time. The phone is such an intimate tool—these texts can shoot right into your heart. I guess there's nothing negative about it, but if she's "dating," then isn't texting me out of bounds? Could she possibly be so coldhearted, all of a sudden, that she could text me for a quick laugh, and that's it? That isn't the Roxy that I know. After everything I've said to her about my feelings and our future? I don't know if I should respond.

4:00 PM

OK, I took an hour and thought about it. I texted her back, "Bags! Bags!" just like I did with "Ubiquitous Zigzags." She did end up coming to my place shortly after that one. We're still connected. I'd tried to separate, but now we're back in digital touch, for the moment, at least. I could hear back from her right away or I could never hear from her again. No idea. This combustion could fuel me or kill me. As hard as I've worked to put love behind me, it's right under the dirt ready to bloom.

If she wants to get together, I'll get dressed up and we'll fuck like it's senior prom. Maybe I should have texted back, "Engagement ring! Engagement ring!" Or maybe I shouldn't have texted back at all. Was I weak or strong, Sheriff?

I wish Stasya were here.

7:00 PM

I went over there to let Nelson out of the crate and walk them. Even though it seems to be working, I can't take having Nelson in there during the day. So when we got back, I let him stay out of it. I left the crate door open, though, to see if he'd maybe hang out in there on his own. I don't know how I'd find that out though. If he holds it until the next walk, then we're really getting somewhere.

Nothing from Roxy.

February 16, 7:30 AM

Bad scene this morning. I'm hungover. Nelson was flipping out. His fur was clumpy and damp. He hadn't made it through the night. He was trapped in there in the damned crate with his own feces and urine.

You've probably seen this same picture. I know from my visitations with Father Will that prisoners fling feces and urine at the guards. Sometimes they accumulate it for several days to make it especially vile. I hope to God that nothing like that ever happened to you. I know it's disgusting to talk about, but it's a fact of life for you and so, by extension, for our whole society.

I'm amazed at what you do. You know what I faced in that crate. I grabbed a set of gloves, then pulled Nelson out of there. I had to walk them quickly before I could bathe him, so we hustled out and took care of business. Lauren wanted to touch noses and bump up against him, but I wouldn't let her. I used to get so angry at Nelson, but I can't anymore. He's seven or eight years old—maybe nine or ten? There's just no way I can teach him how to function differently at this point. He loves the treats like hot dogs, but he won't give up his other habits. He wants it all.

Irene would kill me if she knew what was going on. And it's just another failure anyhow.

I apologized to Nelson all the way through his bath and blow-dry. I couldn't put him back in the crate, so we're on newspapers and the useless Organic Marvel of Lies spray again. Don't know what to do next. I tried to redo the braids, but they were ragged and loose and looked sad.

5:00 PM

I ended up spending the whole afternoon at Irene's with the dogs and my laptop. I had all of the windows open. It was only sixty-two out; we were freezing. I looked at her bedroom. The hardwood floors are as bad as the kitchen was, except it's only the path around the bed. She has a great big old brass bed frame and a very deep mattress and box spring, so the top of it is about four feet in the air. Totally ridiculous.

I wonder if anyone'd ever slept on that bed with her in years gone by. There's a stepladder next to it that she must use to climb up there. How is she going to manage this when she gets back? There are four pillows and the bedspread, all of which are stained and revolting. I'm sure the dogs sleep on there with her. There's one of those half-chairback things with the arms. It looks like it went through a flood.

When she comes back from the convalescent home, she'll be clean, so crawling back onto this bed would be a reversion of tremendous proportion. Her dresser looks antique and very expensive, a leftover from her Beverly Hills days. Unfortunately, the bottom edges and the legs have been destroyed by the dogs, so it's now worthless. There's an Art Deco–type acrylic lamp on her nightstand. Could be from the '40s or '50s, very cool, though it's now dull and yellowed from the fetid air through which its light must fight every evening. I don't know if the lamp can be reclaimed. On a table on the other side of the bed there's a small TV covered with dust. There's an out-of-date cable box and remote. Nothing turns on. Obviously, what she does is read. There are books all over the place. The shelves of the bookcase are in disarray. Books are jammed in and double-stacked. The books on the bottom shelf near the floor have seen their last set of eyes because they've been peed on. Most likely, all the books need to be thrown out. That sucks because it's all very good reading, a lot of classics and the best of the twentieth century. Books are piled on the nightstand, on top of the TV, a few even on the windowsill and covering an entire side of the top of her dresser. The dresser mirror is permafogged and cracked all the way down the left, entirely defeated from its demanding life's work. I stand in front of it, and see my own old age—my father. I shudder and look into the bathroom. Holy cow, that's going to have to wait for another time.

I already had my homemade hazmat suit and scrubbing system at the ready, so cleaning the bedroom floor only took a couple of hours. The unmasked hardwood is actually very nice. It's dark, some kind of mahogany or something. I cleaned up the furniture and organized the books into piles in the front room. We're going to figure out what to do with those when she gets back.

February 17, 12:30 PM

Casino stopped me by my car when I was trying to leave for Ralphs.

"How's it going with the dogs?"

It's taken me five months of writing to explain it to you, Sheriff, how do I update Casino when I'm in a hurry? Plus, I doubted that he cared because if he did, he would have at some point offered to lend a hand.

"They're starting to go outside," I said. "They seem calmer. I've been cleaning Irene's—"

"Wow, is that right?" he said. "I would love to check that out. The dogs do seem calmer when I see them with you, all settled down. Maybe I can do something to help out."

At least he knows I'm not giving tours for free. We'll see.

7:30 PM

I'm not sure what to do. I took Casino over to Irene's apartment this afternoon. The dogs freaked out when they saw him.

"They don't like my size 13 kicks," he said. He bent down to pet them, and they settled. "These dogs are just totally different when they're clean like this. It's amazing. I always ran to wash my hands whenever I touched them before. Oh, and look at how their hair has the braids! They're like little Rastafarians."

"Roxy did that originally," I said. "I've been trying to maintain it, but I'm not as good at it."

"Roxy was here? You didn't tell me that. That's great! When was she here?"

"About a week and a half ago," I said. "It was nice, but she said she's dating now, so—"

"I don't believe that for a second," he interrupted.

This gave me hope. "Why not?"

"She loves you too much to fuck around with that bullshit," he said. "She's just messing with you to get you to step up. That's what you told me she said, right? That part of this was about you having your shit together? Then she's stopping by to check up on you and is kicking up dust by trying to make you jealous."

"The jealousy thing only makes me mad. It doesn't make me want to run to her."

"Doesn't matter to her. She wants to motivate you, and also protect herself in case she doesn't get what she wants," he professored. "Women do this kind of shit all the time. If she didn't want any part of you, why would she give you any attention at all—especially coming over?"

"That's what I thought, initially, but I haven't heard from her since," I said. "Except a text. It's a bunch of games. It's crazy shit, and I don't like it."

"It's always crazy shit. You know anybody whose woman doesn't do crazy shit every once in a while? She wants a certain kind of life. I know she wants it with you, but you've got to show her that you can provide that kind of life."

Casino's on his exer-cycle again.

"Well," I said, "if she'd just stuck by me—a little bit of faith and devotion, you know? Then it wouldn't be so painful, instead of pushing me off the bridge like this. I don't really want to talk about it."

"Don't worry about it, man. She'll be back," he said. "I've seen you guys together. There's nothing like it. You just need to maintain your emotional equilibrium about yourself."

"Yeah, OK," I said, putting as much of an end to the topic as I could inflect.

"I just can't believe my eyes—or my nose," he said, looking around. "I wish you had told me you were doing this. I would have come over to help out."

So, so, so much bullshit. But I didn't care, I was receiving high praise, and I need that so badly these days that I'll even take a blue ribbon of bullshit.

We stepped into the bedroom, and he pointed at a framed black and white photo on the wall, "Isn't that just crazy? I can't believe that was her."

I hadn't noticed it before. Maybe I was too busy looking down, being careful where I stepped. There hung a portrait photograph, matted, in a silver frame, like the old-Hollywood starlet photos that hang above the bar at Formosa. It's a young, beautiful blonde woman with her hair parted in the middle, done up in a bun on top of her head, in a three-quarter pose not looking at the camera. The skin is like moonlight on a quiet lake. Her eyes are looking slightly upward, filled with confidence, as if she is hearing the call of a bright and welcoming future. How they used to light those photos to make them unapologetically superhuman.

As I stepped closer to it, Casino said, "That's Irene. Can you believe it?"

"I can't," I said, and I examined it like Lieutenant Columbo at a murder scene. "The hair, the eyes, and the nose—that's about all I can connect up, she's so heavy and sagging now. Plus, this girl looks pleasant and optimistic. I've only seen Irene frowning and miserable."

"We'll, she's lost a lot," Casino said.

"So I've heard," I said.

"When I first moved in, we used to talk some. But when I sensed the hell-o'-crazy, I stepped back. Plus, I never liked the dogs."

"I can understand that. Wow, this picture is the icing on the Krimpet. She's not just a kid who grew up in Beverley Hills. She was beautiful. Maybe her wild stories about her three marriages are true."

"She says a lot of things that sound unbelievable," Casino said, "but she's had a different kinda run at life. I think there's some truth underneath there." Then he noticed the bedspread. "Wow, this is disgusting."

"I bet there's been some truth underneath there, too."

"You know what," he said, "you've done so much over here, I'm going to buy her a new comforter and bed stuff. Do you know when she's coming back?"

"That'd be great, man," I said. *Sure, Casino can swoop in and spend a little money and have his good deed done in no time*, I thought. "I don't know when she's coming back. I have a feeling it won't be too long though." I said that to hasten the incineration of the bedspread.

Casino stepped over to the dresser and pointed at the half-open top drawer. "Speaking of crazy shit," he said. "Look at this."

Lying there among the faded handkerchiefs, costume jewelry, and some old official-looking papers and photographs was a handgun.

"What is she doing with a gun?"

"Well, she's an old lady—over here all alone," he said.

"But she can't see straight. Or drive straight. How could she shoot anything but a wall?"

"I'm more worried about her," he said.

"What do you mean?"

"Look at this place, and these dogs—well, before you straightened things up," Casino said. "She's obviously depressed. Imagine her sitting up here, no TV, staring at this picture of herself from fifty years ago."

"Jesus," I said.

Casino picked up the gun. It is a revolver. He opened up the chamber and then slapped it closed. "It's a .38, very nice one, too.

Three bullets in it. She had that brain tumor and everything. You don't think she's been thinking about dying for about twenty years now? What does she have to live for?"

I looked at the dogs whom I'd set on the bed. *Three bullets—one, two, and three,* I thought, and I looked at that glamour photograph. I know suicidal thoughts. *Why wouldn't Irene think about it?*

"There's a bagful of bullets in here, too. Wow."

"Does she take antidepressants of any kind?" I asked.

Casino motioned toward her nightstand with the tip of the gun. There was a field of green and brown and red prescription bottles. "I'm sure. See for yourself."

What do I know? I rifled through them. A bottle of Prozac, 80 mg/day, Lexapro, and Ativan. Three bottles of OxyContin.

"Damn, that's a lot of pills."

Casino came over. "'Damn' is right. That's a lot of money sitting there. Those Kickers are 40 mg. They can go for $50 each, and those bottles are full. That's $4,500 looking at you right there."

Forty-five hundred dollars. "She doesn't seem to take them."

"Sure, but the doctor keeps lining them up every month, though, no problem. That's what they all do."

"How do you know the value of these pills?"

"How do you not? I'm a DJ. I hear things."

"She's even hoarding these."

"Old people are amazing, man."

"Forty-five hundred dollars?" I asked, accidentally out loud, the adrenaline of quick money and the risk of street crime popping into my head.

"Hoarders know every single piece of crap they have. She probably taps each bottle and counts to three every night before she goes to sleep."

"Well . . ." I stopped, very close to putting a bottle of Oxy in my pocket. Casino saw it.

"If you take just that one bottle, that's fifteen hundred dollars clean. You know, when you think about it, you deserve to get paid. You've been doing all this work for her—the dogs, the apartment.

You think she's even going to thank you? What're you getting out of this? I've really been wondering that, because it's kind of crazy what all you've been doing."

"Yeah, it's crazy," I said, my hand sweating on the plastic bottle.

"But are you a drug guy? You'd have to be a drug guy and sell to drug dudes, you know."

"I'm not a drug guy. I'm not even a drug dude. I don't know how to sell drugs. I don't even know how to buy them."

"Nathan does. He'd take care of everything. He's not a real drug dude, he's just sick and can't work and getting screwed by the system. You split it with him 60/40. You still come away with like $900."

"You should be a businessman."

"I've been taking business classes at LACC," he said. "Have to expand my knowledge to expand my empire."

"Is Nathan really selling his own prescriptions?"

"He needs the money more than the relief, you know? You need the money, too, right? Some relief?"

Relief, I thought. "So I'd be helping him out in a way."

"You could give half of your cash from it to Irene. Like a Robin Hood. Surprise her, or take the dogs to the vet for some shots or some shit. They're her pills, and the cash would do her way better than those things sitting in the bottle waiting on expiration dates. Plus help yourself, too."

"Why don't you do it then?"

"Not my thing."

"How come I can't just say 'Not my thing'? Because it's not my thing either, you know."

"Well, when you're black, a lot of people just assume that it's your thing, so sometimes you have to point out that it's not your thing. But you don't know yet that it's not your thing, because you've never done it. Experience is the greatest teacher. You know, you're single now, you're a smart guy—you're spending all your time on those dogs when this should be the best, freest time of your life. I'm worried about you."

"So I should take the 'Contin for myself, or sell it."

"I'm not suggesting that at all. I've seen the things turn bad real quick on people—good people. Actually, I think you should just leave things as they are for now. You've been making it work on your own."

"And jail rape feels bad."

"Can't argue with that."

I was more concerned with Irene at that point. *Plenty of people on antidepressants kill themselves*, I thought. I was now deeper into her personal shit than even when I was on my knees on her kitchen floor.

"I hope she's getting help in that home, but Fay says it's awful, and that she hates it," I said. Then, pointing at the pistol, which Casino was still admiring, "Should we empty out that gun? Maybe take the bullets away entirely? Or, at least, put it back in the drawer now?"

Casino put the gun back, saying that he didn't think we should mess with it. She might only have it here for protection, and "If somebody broke in here like they did your place, and she got hurt because she couldn't even get it loaded, then I'd feel terrible."

"Do you own a gun?" I asked.

"Yep," he said. "No one's taking my shit without getting killed."

So, I'm the only one around here who doesn't own a gun, Sheriff. Should I? I did have a break-in. I suppose if I'd decided to change careers and become a drug dealer tonight, then I'd eventually need one. What should I do about it? Three bullets is just a coincidence, right? Who has a half-loaded gun sitting around and three months' worth of OxyContin except Kurt Cobain?

"I hope Irene doesn't want to shoot me for getting rid of her garbage," I said, trying to levitate myself out of this somber fog.

"Ha! She might," Casino laughed. "No, it'll be fine. She's got to be happy about all this."

"She was really angry that Roxy trimmed their hair."

"Oh, Roxy did that, too?" he said, smiling. "She's great. I miss her."

"Well, Casino, you're telling me that everything's going to be fine with both of these women in my life," I said. "What are the chances that you'll be correct?"

"I know women," he said. "Just keep doing what you're doing—you being you—and it'll all work out. No worries."

It's all worries, Sheriff. Me being me? What a terrible plan.

Casino grabbed one of the prescription bottles and shook out a few pills. "Here, take these. One each day for the next three days, and that's it. No more. Enjoy yourself and lighten up a bit. It'll help your knee out, too."

"My knee's been feeling better with all the walking."

"But I know you're in pain in other places. These won't kill you. Trust me. And Irene wouldn't kill me for taking three of her pills. She's offered them to me before when my wrist was bothering me. Three little ones to give yourself a break, maybe to sleep, and that's it."

I brought the whole bottle back with me.

10:00 PM

Nelson and this crate—I can't go in there and pull him out of his own sewage every morning. He wouldn't be learning anything. He has such a sweet, fun, energetic disposition. He jumps straight up and down for treats. I've taught him to stand on his hind legs for them. He smiles at you as he listens to you talk, and his tail flutters like a scolding finger hurrying you along when he's being hooked onto his leash for a walk. Sometimes we run. (I can run now a little bit on my knee, feels good.) He wants to take off and feel some wind against his face. His mouth hangs open, and his tiny pink tongue flaps up against his nose. Lauren is never into it at first, but we drag her along, and she strides up. It strikes me that, with Irene, they've probably never run before—never run. When she comes back, they might never run again. Nelson will leap forward and pull at the leash, but nothing. I can't take that. They'll lose so many things.

I have to stick with the crate, don't I? If I don't believe in him, who will? The answer is later walks at night before he goes in and earlier walks in the morning. We just have to commit.

Lauren barks less because of the amount of exercise she's getting. I may have solved that problem.

February 18, 1:00 PM

Casino came by with the new bedding for Irene. He un-surreptitiously mentioned that he'd spent nearly $300. I could have gotten it all at Ross for eighty bucks. Smartly, he bought dark brown everything. I didn't have the heart to tell him how quickly it'll all be destroyed. It looks way better in there. He threw out all the old stuff. That was nasty work. I give him credit for that.

The only room left to clean is the front room, the living room or—as it feels—the dying room. All the old person mélange gives it a creepy feel, like the parlor of an unlicensed funeral director. The biggest issue is the rug. I'm sure that, like the blue-and-white vase collection, it's from her Beverly Hills days. Even in its molded and torn condition, I'm sure she still sees it as a luxury item. She's kept such a snug grip on her stagnation that any change will likely be traumatic, right? But how do I not do it? How do I stop with what I've done and leave it at a half measure?

Here you go, Irene, the kitchen, the bedroom, and the dogs are good as new, but you still have your living room, which can comfortably represent the haunted recesses of your disturbed mind, to sit in and relax and then be completely consumed by your own apathy.

If I give her any filth option, she'll take it. So I can't. But who am I to be giving her options about anything in her old age? I'm just the neighbor. Ridiculous. Am I the crazy one? Am I the one with the obsession? Why have I focused so and set such extreme goals in all of this when what I should have been doing since Roxy left me is working on ways to improve myself and my own life? I should have done what Casino did, just spend $300 on miscellany and walk away guilt free. If I had $300, I would've spent it on antibarking paraphernalia to begin with for Sophie (Satan torment her soul). Though, I have to admit, even with all the frustrations, working with those two dum-dums has been about the only thing that I've enjoyed in the last five months. And, sort of, with you.

What would I have gotten paid to do all of this, even just to walk and feed the dogs for all these weeks? Here I am piss poor, struggling for every stupid penny, and I've soaked so much time and attention into this project as if it mattered. What a stupid choice. Look at what I'm doing. "Know thyself"—the oracle of Delphi. I'd rather know someone else.

8:00 PM

I should "assume the best, rather than the negative," Ally preaches to me.

"OK—Irene'll come home, be thrilled with the transformation in her apartment, become overwhelmed with gratitude, will kiss me on the cheek and promise to take great care of the dogs and her surroundings from now on. Yep—with a brand-new bum arm on top of the blind eye, deaf ear, half-dead face, the vertigo, and the hoarding OCD."

"Yes, Richard, think positive."

February 19, 11:00 AM

I got a phone message from Irene today. She thanked me for watching the dogs, actually made a little joke about their hair (which shows she hasn't forgotten about it), asked me to give them hugs for her, and told me that she may be home in a week or so, maybe even sooner.

My heart sunk—which surprised me. *It's all going to be over soon,* I thought. It's been fifty-three days since she fell. These dogs feel like they're mine. They depend on me. And the work's not done. The living room isn't clean. Nelson isn't ready. Lauren is so close. If I hand them back this way, then Nelson's bacchanalian ways will take over the whole apartment again because she won't clean up after him, unless I tell her to.

I've got to get Nelson over the hump. If we do have one more full week, then maybe the crate and tons of walks with Treats for Pee can work their magic. Papillon never broke, but we might be able to turn Nelson.

I'm not going to lie to you, Sheriff, I'm going to miss these guys. The pride in Nelson's eyes as he chomps down a well-earned treat has become a nutrient to me. I pat him on the head and tell him he's a big boy, and he says, *I feel like a big boy,* and his tail buzzes back and forth. He's going to lose that when she gets back. She'll cuddle him when he's on her lap, but these dogs want some parameters of behavior, a regimen to follow. They're happier the new way with some exercise. They need someone in their lives to follow and share their joy and accomplishments. Life is more than just being on someone's lap.

Irene said they want her to start using a walker, and she asked if I would "bring the dogs over" so that she could "practice walking them with the walker down the hallway."

Did I hear that right? Yes, I did. Do you think I said yes? Do you think I could have said no? I'm just going to try to avoid it until she gets home.

I wish Roxy would call. I need someone to help me power through this. And to sit on my lap.

February 20, 10:20 AM

Time to get serious. I'm going to bring the dogs over to my apartment for these last few days. I'm going to keep Nelson in the crate all day, but I'll be here to keep him company. This has to kick up to intensive training. I'll check in with Austen. The trick will be keeping an eye on Lauren so that she doesn't go inside. She's been doing really well on our walks, so I think I can trust her. I'd hate to leave her alone at Irene's while Nelson is here with me. I think we can handle this. I'm going to get up every morning before the crack of dawn, rush them outside, and then I'm going to walk them every two hours on the nose to head off any accidents or rebellion. It'll be difficult, but, like a surgeon on call, I'll just have to be ready and vigilant at all times, rested or weary.

2:30 PM

I found the answer. At Tailwaggers, resupplying myself with Organic Marvel for my own apartment, I saw these nylon dog houses. They're soft-sided "dog homes," they call them. They're less Rikers Island than the metal crates. I bought one large enough to hold both dogs. It cost sixty-five dollars, about the same as a cheap dinner date, but since I have none of those happening anymore, I figured I could swing it on a credit card. As had Austen, the saleslady swore that the dogs would not pee inside there. It's bright blue with black mesh windows and a zippered door. It looks like camping gear. When I was a kid, it would have been an adventure to sleep in there. I'm going to use peer pressure, keeping Lauren in there with him. There's no way Nelson will mess up a small space that both dogs are in, right?

Also, Fay called already to pester me about taking the dogs to help with Irene's "walker practice."

"Can you possibly do it, Fay? I'm really busy."

"Oh, I'm afraid if something happened, I wouldn't be able to control the dogs like you can."

So I'm stuck.

7:00 PM

Moving day: I put the camper together—I call it the Dignity Box—and brought them over with their bowls, food, and the remainder of Irene's newspapers, just in case. Fed them dinner, walked. Now we're here.

February 21, 10:00 AM

Having them here is an intense distraction. I'm so paranoid about an accident that I keep turning around in my chair and looking at them, even when they're asleep. Stressful.

2:20 PM

It's amazing how much they sleep. How was Sophie barking for so many hours? Her internal chaos must have been like the fission of atomic isotopes.

I'm sitting here, watching these two dum-dums sleeping up against each other, Nelson's tongue hanging out, their breathing synchronized, an occasional leg twitch from a dream off in their Lilliputian world. Their eyes squint closed when they sleep, like they're working really hard at it.

I don't feel as much stress anymore. I've decided I'm not going to abandon them at that point, no matter how angry or freaked out Irene may be. I'm not going to just toss the dogs back in there and slam her door shut.

I can't believe I'm saying it, but they're part of me. So I have to have a relationship with Irene. Maybe she'll let me help out with them. I think about that gun, and I wonder if I should try to cajole her into giving it to me for safekeeping. Does her doctor know she has a gun in her bedroom? Does Fay know? Do you have any advice on that? If she says it's for protection, then I'll just promise to protect her. We'll cross that bridge when we stumble there.

I'm imagining that I'll be able to have conversations with Irene when she may not even be grateful for the favor I've done. She didn't care about me when Sophie was around, why would she now? People can be selfish when they want to be left alone. I'm learning to not have expectations. You can't think anyone will behave the way that you would in any given situation. Look at Roxy. Instead of running away from our problems, I wanted to work on them. She felt that being away was best. Either way would have been difficult. I think her way inflicted more pain, but it's what forced me to look at my own life as I have, so maybe it was right. Plus, I have to let her be who she is if I'm going to love her no matter how things turn out. And I need to figure out who I am before she can completely love me. Should the word *completely* be put with the word *love*? Do we ever figure out who we are?

Your whole life must be a struggle against expectations, Sheriff. Every bad person you meet on calls must behave in despicable ways that blow your mind. I wonder how much control you try to exert over your children, if you have any, or your wife. I'd think it'd be tough not to, given the havoc you deal with on the job. How do you separate your power circumstances? I wish I had power circumstances—just one, even. I think Roxy disliked my lack of power and assertion. I had that when I played music. But eventually I saw myself as a victim of everything. In many ways, I was, but now I'm going to fix that by involving myself in the havoc and trying to clear things up.

Speaking of havoc, I'm thinking of going back to teaching. I'm more mature now. I was good at it. I could use the benefits, the retirement plan, and the stability. Maybe the dream I want now is to be settled and secure like what Roxy wants. Instead of being defensive, I need to see that she's someone who loves me and wants what's best for me. I've been afraid of really trying to be a provider because nothing financially for me has ever worked out. Slow and steady might be a better way to go.

All this from watching the dogs sleeping together in their camper. They have no idea.

9:30 PM

Nelson pooped four times today. I've started a chart in a notebook. That's the problem that I've been missing all this time. He needs to go way more often than I ever thought. He might need four or five walks a day. He seems perfectly healthy and content. He either needs these walks, or he's become desperately addicted to treats. Nelson's lifestyle really should be reversed—outside walking all day and only brought inside to relax three or four times. I'm going to keep track of this, the way a nurse jots things down on a clipboard at the foot of a patient's bed. Maybe I'll show it to Austen.

I'm creating a clinical study, and if it bears out that Nelson needs this many walks, then I'll have the numbers to show Irene to let her know what her responsibilities are. She can take that knowledge and do whatever she's going to do with it, but it would be a heck of a life choice to ignore the data that I'm compiling.

February 22, 3:00 PM

Day two with the Dignity Box. They're already accustomed to it. I let them out to sit in the living room for short periods during the day. Because we're walking so frequently, I'm confident that they're wrung dry by the time they get back inside.

Nelson loves to sleep on the couch. He's got such an interesting personality. He loves to jump and play, but he also likes his alone time. He wanders off and finds a place to curl up, facing away from you as if he just wants to sit and think, undisturbed.

Lauren, on the other hand, cannot stand not being on my lap. First, she sits by my chair and stares up at me. Then, when the lonely eyes haven't worked, she stands on her hind legs, paws at the seat, and squeals as if her heart is being ligatured. When she doesn't see a lap, she's perfectly fine. But as soon as my thighs are parallel to the floor, she can't take it. So, I let her sit with me while I work. Her whole body goes limp, entirely submissive, very sweet. If she could purr, she would. She doesn't fidget around, or nudge at me, or insist on being petted. She respects the privilege and knows well enough not to be pushy. That's how we spend the afternoons—Lauren with me, and Nelson off thinking, wrestling with the great imponderables of infinite dog space.

5:00 PM

We saw Austen this afternoon as soon as we stepped outside for our walk. He was across the street in front of the school. I scooted back inside to grab the notebook with the Nelson chart in it so that I could show it to him and see what he thought.

Austen waved lightly, not lifting his hand above his waist as we crossed the street. His usually bright posture was gone, his shoulders sloped, and his wrists were loose as he held his dogs' leashes.

After a quick greeting, he just said it: "Misty died last night."

"Oh no. Oh no. I'm so sorry."

Though we hardly know each other, he was comfortable enough to weep in front of me, which made me feel close to him. Blue tears welled behind his glasses.

"She wasn't feeling well. I took her to the vet, and he found a tumor on her lung. Cancer. It'd already spread to her liver. This kind of thing can happen with Labs, but you don't think about it."

"I'm so sorry."

"There's a surgery, but it's so invasive, and it creates, like, a yearlong process, and it's horrible for the dog, so it was a terrible couple of days."

You could feel the empty leash with us there.

"She was our leader dog. These guys don't quite know what to do without her."

Nelson, Lauren, and I walked with them the rest of the way. It was quiet and slow. The dogs all knew. We did chat. We managed to chuckle about the chart. He said that Nelson was fine, normal. I gave Austen my number and said he could call anytime. I don't want his eating disorder to strike again. And Austen was still in pain from his boyfriend.

This is one of the reasons, Sheriff, that I've never owned a dog and don't want to. It's too short a time span, and it's way too difficult at the end. I don't know how people do it. At the same time, Nelson and Lauren, the enthusiasm with which they grab each day, already is pretty great to wake up to.

February 23, 11:45 AM

I got the annual West Hollywood neighborhood street parking permit renewal form in the mail today. Again. It reminds me that I might live here, in this apartment, in this situation, for another whole year, or forever. I get the new permit, scrape the old one off the windshield with a razor blade—why do you make them so difficult to remove?—then put the new one on, the new year staring me in the face. Roxy'd made a snide comment last year when I handed her the updated guest pass for her rearview mirror, a red one replacing the pink one, and it turned into a fight.

"Committed to another year, are you?" She was holding a veritable "red flag" in her hand.

"It's the law," I said. I was being cute, but all she heard was my personal Law of Inertia, and she was giving me a hefty fine for a nonmoving violation. Also, Sheriff, trying to be cute is a low-percentage way to avoid a fight.

She said that I was consumed by a "myopic derangement" with this apartment and Sophie, and that I probably wanted to be here forever, "swallowed up by the ethos of my own complaining."

What she should have done was to tell me that she could compromise for the greater good of us being together. She could have rescued me from this place with love and support.

"Why don't you move in here with me?" I must have suggested that a hundred times. "With the money we'd each save, we'd both be working our way out of debt in no time."

"This place isn't even large enough to hold you and your complaints," she said, "let alone me and everything of mine."

"I'll put most of my shit in my half of the garage in back. I'll put an armoire in the living room for my clothes, and you can have the whole bedroom closet."

"It's too small. And we're too old for that kind of life."

"Let's make it just for a year then. Twelve months. At the end of each month, we go to a nice romantic dinner where we drink wine and write our rent checks and celebrate the money we're saving. Then we go get an apartment with cash in hand."

Ally'd thought that was a reasonable plan, but Roxy wouldn't budge for a budget. Hey, she's worked hard. She doesn't want to feel like her life is going backward. I think she became an observer of the relationship as opposed to a partner in it.

"I know plenty of couples who've sacrificed space for a while in order to be able to save some money or pay off some bills," I said.

"Those days are long gone for me. That's not charming anymore, Richard."

9:00 PM

I think about the gun over there and wonder if I should just take it. Just put my foot down and say, "Crazy old ladies should not have loaded guns."

I did take one of the OxyContin pills a couple of days ago. Didn't really do much, helped me sleep, but I need to get up early for the dogs anyway, so I'm going to put back the remaining ones.

Fay called me again to ask about taking the dogs to the nursing home and doing the walker test.

About a year after my father's stroke, I coached him back to driving during a spring break. I took him to an empty parking lot and showed him that he could do it using his left hand and left foot. He eventually had his mechanic friend cobble up an illegal pedal extender that moved the gas from the right to the left of the brake. That gave him a ticket to limited freedom, to actually get back to Chick's occasionally. It brought him some joy. But Irene with the walker and the two dogs? It's the bridge at Arnhem.

February 24, 7:30 PM

The chart is unbelievable. Nelson is a hyperdigestive machine.

9:50 PM

Nelson had an accident in the Dignity Box when I was out. Had to scrub it down again with soap and a brush and hose outside. He's not going to learn. There aren't enough treats in the world. The only option left would be to lace them with cocaine so a manic addiction could drive his need to get outside. He's energetic enough without it. Poor thing. He's just a little too old and beyond the rainbow. Or I wasn't a good enough teacher. Irene's going to be home any day, and this has all been a failure.

February 25, 5:00 PM

Having the dogs here has definitely helped me break Lauren of her barking when other dogs walk by out front. I use an empty Bud Light can with a bunch of pennies in it, something poor Austen had suggested.

"A couple of shakes as soon as she barks," he'd explained. "It jolts their attention away from what they were barking at."

She hates it but is already associating it. I'm making a note to give the penny can to Irene. It will be her welcome home gift. Hopefully one of her arms will be strong enough to shake it. I may have solved the barking without you, Sheriff. What do you think of that?

Speaking of giving Irene things, am I supposed to have flowers for her or something?

11:45 PM

Only a few days left, I guess. At night now, I pull the Dignity Box into the bedroom. They've spent enough nights on their own after all these weeks. It's always tough to corral them into it because they want to get up on the bed so badly. They reach up to the bed with their arms, which I guess are legs, but they seem more like arms, with the pleading in the eyes and the whole act.

When I finally do get them into their camper, Nelson curls up, but Lauren sits there staring at me through the mesh door like a little Emily Dickinson, writing poems about death and immortality. She winces in tiny whispers as she reads one aloud. She's brilliant. Sometimes she pants to notch up the tension. If Nelson wakes during the night, he gently paws at the mesh as if to point out to me that it's in the way. Their eyes reflect a glint of the bare, dark streetlight that cheats into the room and beam it at me, so much so that I can feel it even when my eyes are closed. Sometimes it's an entire hour that they'll both sit there looking at me, hoping to get in the bed, absolutely confident that I'll change my mind about the separation.

It's tough to stay disciplined. I'm lonelier than they are.

February 26, 10:20 AM

This chart is amazing, Sheriff. It really tells the tale. I feel like Jane Goodall. I hope Irene takes to it.

Speaking of, I suppose I should take them in and help Irene with the walker practice.

4:00 PM

OK, I did it. Nursing homes are so difficult to walk through. All I could think about was my mom and dad. Those poor old folks in there, and a couple young ones, too, soldiers I assume. One man with just one limb, his right arm, sat in a wheelchair in the hallway watching people go by. He wore a stocking cap and had a robe tucked around himself. He had thick brown hair, a mustache and beard, maybe twenty-six years old. He seemed so strong, still a bear of a man. I don't know why they would have him there surrounded by so many endings-in-progress and overt dementia. I carried the dogs in my arms both facing forward, their heads bobbing slowly against my chest as they looked left and right, smiling at everyone. Those who were sentient gave them a big smile back and lots of waves. The soldier grinned and chuckled as we stopped and said hello.

Irene was tickled to see the dum-dums, though she managed to throw in plenty of shots about their shorter hair. "I can barely look at Nelson without his special whiskers." They aren't whiskers, that's hair.

The Nazi was gone, and her bed was empty. Irene said they had to move her to a more secure room. On the third bed was an aged woman, lying still, her blanket pulled up to her chin, staring up at the corner where the walls met the ceiling.

"Martha is ninety-six," Irene said. "She goes in and out, but when she's with it, she's very nice. Too bad her daughter isn't here, you'd like her. She's pretty."

"Did Martha happen to have her when she was sixty-six years old, by any chance?"

I set Nelson up onto Irene's chest, and they kissed like lost lovers. Irene stretched her leg to pet Lauren with her bare foot at the end of the bed, but I kept shifting the poor thing away from Irene's hospital feet.

Irene had a hard time getting out of the bed. She has no strength in her right arm, and not much anywhere else, plus still lots of soreness. Apparently, there were cracked ribs as well, but they do nothing for those. She was very shaky once she stood. When we got into the hallway, I saw no walker.

"Oh, I can't use that contraption and still walk the dogs."

"But that's what you told me we were going to practice."

"I just want to show them that I can do it so that they'll let me go home."

She decided in that moment that we were at our starting line in the middle of the hallway. No one seemed to care that the four of us were about to launch and crash. I handed her the leashes, and she immediately complained: "I don't know how I'm going to walk them with these things. Where are mine?"

"How can the leashes matter? These're good ones," I said, now in concert with all the other visitors who were there in the home, busily deciphering nonsense with their delusionary loved ones.

We started forward, the dogs in different directions, and their leashes wrapped right around Irene's ankles. She went on, oblivious.

"Stop. Stop," I said in a panic. "Where are the nurses or the aides? This is nuts. I can't guide you or keep you from falling here."

"I'm fine."

"I'm not. This is crazy. You're not strong enough for this, or balanced. The dogs are going to pull you right down, and you're going to end up here for another seven weeks."

An aide deciphered my raised voice from the babel of the regular patients and came fast-paced to us. But instead of talking sense to Irene, she crouched down to adore the dogs. Then two more aides came, and two more, and two more, and the dogs were swarmed. Against my objections, our group eventually began shuffling down the hallway all together like pallbearers for the pope. It looked like a walking group hug. It didn't last ten feet.

"You can't do this," an aide name-tagged Marisa said. "It's too crazy." Then she motioned toward me. "Can't your son take care of the dogs for a while?"

Irene and I simultaneously protested: "I'm not her son." / "He's not my son."

"Irene," Marisa said, "why are you doing this? You know this is too much."

"It's the leashes—"

"It's not the leashes," I said.

"Why don't we all sit down," Marisa suggested, and we made our way to two chairs in the hallway. Irene and I sat down. I took back control of the dogs. Marisa and what was probably the entire staff left us there to work it out.

"How do you think that went, Irene?" I started.

"It was fine. Lauren is a little jumpy. I think she's forgotten me."

"Everything about that whole snafu was jumpy. I'm glad your arm is healing, but you didn't fall because of your arm. You're still having balance issues, I think, and you need to take your time. You should be trying one of those rolling chair walkers or a cane. My father used one of those with the four-pronged bottom."

"I can't. My hands aren't strong enough to use the brakes or even to lean on a cane."

Old people don't like to be juxtaposed with dead people.

"We'll—"

"Can you put Nelson on my lap, please? I miss him so much, I'm ready to crack."

I did, and then we sat in a prolonged silence among the clouds of the home's normal bedlam. Occasionally staff or patients would wheel or walker by and coo over the dogs. Irene would mention that their hair is "supposed to be long," but that they look great. Nelson's tongue hanging out was spreading lots of joy. I eventually excused myself because we weren't going to silently contemplate until a resolution was reached.

I carried the dogs out. We stopped when we saw the soldier. He laughed at Nelson and petted Lauren on the chest. "Hi, little girl." We nodded at one another, and I said, "Take care."

6:00 PM

Launderland is the saddest place in the world. You know the one, the Laundromat in the small strip mall up on Santa Monica Boulevard at Hayworth, next to the 7-Eleven and Los Tacos. Roxy loved doing laundry. You couldn't keep her away from a fresh pile of warm clothing to fold and put away. I took bags over to her place most of the time, and she'd dive on it. Launderland used to be only for emergencies or for when she was out of town.

Roxy has a few quirky allergies and sensitivities. One of them is dyes and perfumes in laundry detergent. The day when I knew I was in love with her was when I bagged up all of my clothing, all of my bedding—sheet sets, pillows, blankets, comforter—every towel and washcloth in my apartment—and hauled the lot of it to Launderland to wash fragrance- and dye-free in case Roxy started staying over at my place, and maybe grabbing something of my clothes to wear, which I wanted so badly. I pictured her in my T-shirts, my dress shirts, my pajamas. I couldn't wait. I took up twenty-two washers that afternoon. Likely a record. The locals were in awe. One woman said that it was the most romantic gesture she'd ever seen. It took me over two hours to fold everything and put it all away. Roxy teared up and kissed me when I told her. It was like a massive bouquet of unscented flowers. Our first overnight here was amazing.

That makes Launderland all that more difficult. KRTH, the radio station they play there, is always dialing up sad songs. That, along with the dull, lonely hum of the machines, like wounded soldiers moaning on a battlefield, and the grinding gloominess in the cacophony of chemical perfumes, remind me that I still use fragrance-free Tide in hopes that Roxy and her allergies will one day be back.

There was an indecently cute girl there today. Straight brown hair to her shoulders, tied back for chores, thin with a well-bought chest, long legs, nice and athletic looking. She was wearing a white T-shirt, black yoga pants, little blue cross-trainers, white-rimmed sunglasses perched on her head—perfect L.A. laundry-day cute. So perfect, in fact, that I found it difficult to fathom that her clothes ever actually do get dirty. Where did she come from? How is it possible she's alone? Then I recognized her as the yoga pants girl I'd embarrassed myself to during a dog walk. She's brilliantly forceful in her use of those yoga pants, and thank God for it. She had her fluffy white Larry Tate dog with her, tied to a bench.

Ally keeps telling me to move on, so I thought I'd see what I could do. Our washes were on opposite ends of the cycle—my dryers finishing as she was putting her clothes into her washers. I decided to take my time and wait out the twenty-six minutes until her final spin. I sat down with my book. I'm reading *Selected Stories of Anton Chekhov*. I should have been reading something more upbeat. Chekhov's world is as cold and gray as laundry water before the rinse. Not right for love at Launderland.

I should have told myself that the fragrances from the detergents were from flowers breezing in a garden, a perfect place for this young lady and me to find each other, but I didn't. I just sat there pretending to read Chekhov. My dryers finished spinning. I got up and checked them and pretended to be perturbed that my clothes weren't dry enough yet, and then plunked in quarter after quarter, risking the shrinking of my clothes down to G.I. Joe doll size.

Turned out that I was better at waiting for her to come over than at trying to talk to her. Waiting is all I do. Truth is, I'm still waiting for Roxy—I want to be finishing her dryers—and I don't even want to talk to another woman until I finally find out if there's going to be a second chance. Looking at this girl felt like cheating. What if I did get a date with her? I'd lose interest as soon as Roxy called, if she calls. Is this sad? What opportunities am I letting pass by?

Anyhow . . . it's not like I have my shit together yet or anything. I'd only be presenting the same lost, miserable, problem child to Yoga Pants, or any other girl, until something changes for me. And yes, of course I'm scared of rejection. Might as well take care of that on my own before anyone else has to bother doing it.

9:00 PM

Remember the story of Jonah and the whale? The Bible thing? Well, fish—Jonah and the fish. Everybody has a version of it—Judaism, Islam, Christianity. It was Jonah and the great fish or "huge fish" originally, but after tripping through several languages, "huge fish" got translated into "whale," which, ironically, is a swimming mammal and not a "huge fish." But it was huge enough to swallow a man whole (a lucky man, unlike Captain Quint in *Jaws*). Of all the stories about miracles, Jonah was the one as a kid that made me doubt the whole "testament" aspect behind Bible writing. I think writing a Bible these days would be much more challenging. But Jonah, inside the body of a whale, with little else to do or even room to move around much, prayed to God to get the whale to let him go, not eat him, as it were, pause its digestive enzymes long enough to get bored with his prey, perhaps desire to yawn and thereby allowing Jonah freedom to escape back into the sea, where presumably he'd be rescued by an animal-skin-wearing early *Baywatch* crew.

I feel like I've been swallowed by a giant Yorkie. Well, a giant Yorkie would actually just be the size of a regular dog, so let's say a gigantic giant Yorkie. And it smells inside. And I have no room to move or think, just lie awake, sleepless, and to talk to you. Think about talking to you, pretend that I am. And think that I can talk to Roxy. Think-talk through so many pretend conversations, until I'm swallowed up or spit out—onto the street or to whatever point upon this vast sea on which we've drifted.

9:40 PM

Roxy texted just now, just a little "how r u?" line. It turned into a quick texting conversation. She said she wants to get together to talk—tomorrow. What should I do? I don't want to sit with her and have her tell me how happy she is now, if she is, and that she wants to forge a friendship with me.

I can't handle being friends with her just yet. What do friends talk about? Relationships, who they're dating, getting laid? I don't want that. I suppose she just wants to peek in again. But what for? Maybe she doesn't even know.

February 27, 4:00 PM

Thank God I have these dogs to walk to burn off some energy. Meeting Roxy tonight. We still haven't come down on a place to meet up. Been cleaning my place, hunting down any dog smell.

February 28, 5:45 PM

Roxy spent the night.

We met for drinks at the Village Idiot on Melrose, which is closer to my place than hers, which I found interesting to begin with. She was dressed casually—jeans, low boots, and a blouse—nothing forcefully alluring, yet tight enough around her breasts with three buttons undone so I could see the beginning of the trail toward everything I'd lost. She did have her "evening out" makeup on, however, unlike the day we broke up, or the time I saw her after. And she smelled like night jasmine after a breezy rain. She ordered her pinot noir and teased me about the way that I always ask the bartender for a beer recommendation because I never know what I want. But it wasn't the eye-rolling, exasperated teasing of our last months together. She joked with a refreshed smile, the one that used to get such a kick out of my quirks. In fact, I was the one struggling to be comfortable. *What's happening? Am I just the object of her rejection? Am I an injured mouse to a house cat?* I didn't know what to say, when I should be forcing a smile, or even how to sit and look natural on a barstool. I ordered a Manhattan.

I wanted no talking. I wanted her on my lap. I wanted a long kiss to ford the icy river. I wanted her breasts in my hands, her warm thighs on mine, our bodies together to speak for all the apologies. Words were negotiation. She held control because she'd broken up with me. She was either moving on or coming back. She was judging me. I didn't have the fortitude to reciprocate. It was too intoxicating to be near her to have any judgment or reason. Her eyes were my blue planet again.

I shouldn't have wanted to kiss her, or talk, or even be there. But I knew that if I could laugh and make her laugh, I'd seem fine—a simple trick to life I'd learned to get by when I was a kid. And it wasn't very difficult. I joked about the dogs, the Dignity Box, and Lauren's late-night tragic poems. After a couple glasses of wine, she asked if she could see the dogs again.

Last time she was here, she gave lots of attention to the dogs but turned me into a pillar of salt when she told me that she was dating.

As we got ready to leave the bar, I thought, *How dare she do this? How can she be around me and have surgically eliminated all romantic and sexual feelings? And to stick this friendship attitude in my face?* As I signed the check, my hand shook like it was tapping out Morse code from the signal room on the *Titanic*. Every cell in my body was jumping with sexual energy, battling to be first to be touched by her again, but my bones were chilled with insecurities, and my heart was screaming like a Stuka dive bomber. Everything was subtracting up in my head. Nothing in my life has changed for the better. I have nothing to impress her with. I haven't even painted a room, or gotten new sheets, or a shower curtain, or something. And I certainly don't have anything that might make her jealous. All I've done this whole time was to sit, paralyzed like my stroked-out father, waiting for her or death, and complaining to you about the dogs, who very possibly might have both shit in their Dignity Box by the time we get back.

It turned out they were fine. They were ecstatic to see me, like villagers greeting Jesus after he'd raised Lazarus from the grave, and likely they were surprised to see another human being entering our dungeon.

Roxy immediately picked up Nelson and practically cuddled the sacs out of his lungs. I don't know what it is about Nelson that captures women's hearts so. It was even the same when he was still grubby. The tongue. Maybe it's because he's a male who can't talk. Actually, I do think that's what it is. He's had to learn to communicate solely with his eyes, and it speaks across species.

I warned her that this was typically a crisis moment in the needing-a-walk schedule, so the four of us leashed up and stepped out in the quiet and cool night air. God, we felt like the perfect nuclear family. *How can she not feel it?*

As angry as I am about the breakup, and as resentful as I am with my thoughts of abandonment, judgment, and jealousy, I couldn't help but feel warm and safe out there. I watched her ass wiggle as Nelson took her darting ahead. Maybe it was just wine-wonderful, I don't know, but Roxy has a way about her that when she stops and remarks about the stars, you can't help but wonder if the stars aren't saying the same things about her.

When Nelson stopped to go, I told Roxy about the chart. She couldn't stop laughing. It reminded her of our rummy score book. Yes, the chart—and I—are ridiculous.

"He goes four times a day?" she asked. "No wonder Irene's place was so awful. She can't keep up with that."

"That's the benefit of science," I said. "Now I have the research to prove it. She's going to have to step up—and soon."

"You're going to be heartbroken to let them go," she said. "I can tell. You love these guys, don't you?"

What an unfortunate grouping of words there. Was she just being clueless, Sheriff? "*Heartbroken . . . let go . . . love*"? She'd taken a billy club to the innocent butterflies in my stomach. We were standing in the same spot where, several weeks ago, she'd announced to me that she was dating. But no one had asked me, to this point, if I'd loved the dogs. I hadn't thought about quantifying something that had started out as a knee-deep swamp I'd been bumbling through.

She cradled Nelson, and the two sets of eyes begged me for a response. I picked up Lauren and held her against my chest.

"These two dum-dums? Well, I love it when they behave," I said. Then Lauren stretched her neck and licked my chin, cleaning the bullshit off my face. Roxy and Nelson laughed at me together.

We came back inside, and Roxy suggested we open a bottle of wine.

"My bottle is a box from Trader Joe's."

"That'll do just fine," she said.

I loved having her here. I loved being around her. She is now the air in here. I hate that she's gone. But I couldn't get myself to be in the present to enjoy it. My mind was scrambling in a battle of Everything That Was versus Everything That Might Be—in the artillery phase—the infantries had yet to crawl forward for the real killing.

This glass of wine put her beyond the limit for driving. She'd made a choice. What'd gotten us this far was that we hadn't talked about "us." We just talked by way of little updates—plenty of Steelers, politics, school, friends, stuff we already agree on. But an eight-ton circus elephant danced in the room on its hind legs juggling flaming barrels of hot dogs, and we ignored it. Maybe it was the dum-dums that kept us calm.

After that wine, she wanted to peer through the looking glass again. We went over to Irene's. The place is 99 percent done. The old odors exist now only in sense memory. The dogs hadn't even been in there for a week.

Roxy couldn't believe it.

"I'm proud of you," she said, and she kissed me. It could have been just a pride kiss though. Hard to tell. She probably felt my trembling as I kissed her back carefully, a thank-you-for-the-pride-kiss kiss.

Stasya would say, "You have the power. You are the man."

Maybe it's not about power, Stasya. I just want her back.

My mind was still made up. It was in her court to change things back. My stomach felt like it was boiling oil. I kept my hands in my pockets to hide them shaking. I hadn't seen this mercurial side of Roxy as something so dangerously unpredictable when I knew it within the confines of a relationship. The capriciousness was cute. It was quirky. It was fun to be spontaneous and change our minds. I just never thought it could go as deep as to devotion.

We came back over here, and sat on the couch to drink more wine and watch TV. *Rear Window* was on Turner.

Roxy laughed, "Imagine how James Stewart'd feel if he saw Irene's apartment through those binoculars."

"It'd be way more shocking than seeing just a stupid murder," I said. "Too much for audiences of that time to handle."

There we were, sitting close on the sofa, looking at each other, laughing. Roxy'd kicked off her boots. Her feet were in my lap. She brought the dogs up to the couch. She couldn't get enough of them. "Nelson, Nelson . . . Nelson, Nelson, Nelson," she'd say, nuzzling her nose against his forehead. He looked at her the way I did, as if she were the most important woman in the world. How did he know?

"His paws are so tiny," she said. "When you brush the hair out of the way and really see them, you can't believe he can even support himself. So freakin' cute."

I didn't understand what was happening. It seemed so intimate to me, but I didn't want to jump to any conclusions. If I leaned over the cliff to kiss her and she pulled away, I'd be rejected all over again. Do you have any idea how many times I told myself to play it cool?

"I'm glad Irene didn't break her leg," I said, referencing the movie. "She'd be utterly helpless."

"Do you know anything about when she'll be back?"

"Any day, maybe tomorrow even."

"Oh no, then you have to give them back."

"Ha, yeah. Then, who knows."

"They adore you," she said, but what her eyes were saying was *I adore you*.

I kissed her. And I was right. Her rich, soft, giving lips extinguished all of the anxiety of the past six months, even the year, and gave me life again in an instant. I was whole again, as Aristophanes would explain it—my other half was found. This is right. Love is right. Holding on had been right. Pain, for both of us, had been a teacher, and pain had been right.

She stayed the night. There is no heroin like the sheer stark beauty of being inside the woman you love. Aloneness is gone forever, and a bright energy pulls you toward the future. Then she insisted on having the dogs up on the bed with us.

In an instant, I'd gone from sleeping alone to having little space for myself. *"They adore you,"* I thought to myself. And then I realized that Nelson snores a little bit. His head was on my pillow. With no vocal chords, it's just tiny breathing sounds, like a mouse with a slight cold. About as damn adorable as anything I'd ever heard.

The dogs made it through the night without any accidents, thank God. I hadn't said anything, but Roxy had no idea what a leap of faith she'd taken by welcoming them up there. I have to say, they did come through. And thank goodness I'm still using hypoallergenic laundry detergent.

In the morning, we were simply happy. No analyzing, no discussion. We walked the dogs and stopped for coffee at the Commissary on Fairfax. We enjoyed the cool and cozy morning, sitting side by side on a bench with the dum-dums warming our laps, making fun of people walking by—especially ones who looked like their dogs. We were back to being Stiller and Meara, nothing but silliness and joy. Life can be easy.

Her phone did buzz a couple of times. She glanced toward her purse but never reached for it.

And then she left. The endorphins lasted about six hours until they burned off, and I crumbled. Do I even ask her what she's thinking? I'm too afraid for that—that buzzing phone. Life is basically Take It or Leave It. She was able to Leave It. How would I know that she wouldn't leave again like Ally fears? Take It and Leave It. There are no guarantees. You know what? I could have left these dogs in the mess they were in, or I could have taken them to the pound where they'd have been fed and out of my hair. But I didn't. I stuck with them. Roxy didn't stick with me.

I guess I shouldn't think about it.

1:00 AM

Maybe I don't want this in my life. Maybe the fact that Roxy left should be enough for me to know that she's not the one. When I think about these dogs—and no, humans aren't dogs—but they are something I think Roxy is not, and that is . . . devoted. Even if it's naive, Nelson and Lauren are a simplified life of unconditional love and loyalty. They give back as much as they can, and they never waver. Is it that the first time I'm truly being loved is by these animals?

Life is more complicated than that, I know. But isn't it also just as simple? If what Roxy truly wanted was to be with me, then she never should have left my side, good or bad. If one of the issues is where my life is at, then get on board, and let's figure this out together. I'd certainly helped her through rough times, and life will bring both of us much bigger challenges down the road. Maybe only now I'm figuring out what commitment is.

I can't believe I'm thinking this, Sheriff, but my mind is changing. I can't have this Roxy heartache hanging over me like this, and I'm not sure if I want her back. Last night was so perfect in so many ways—except that it ended, and for the circumstance that created it—and that can't be removed. Now she drifts in and out like a fog in a graveyard.

I know, I know—she and I need to talk.

March

March 1, 8:30 PM

Hoarders pile up junk for protection the way a dog crawls into a small space during a thunderstorm. Irene now has lots of open space to hide from. Roxy thinks she's going to freak after having her things thrown away without warning (she of the Breakup Bags herself). I'm no psychologist. I don't want her reaching for that gun. I am the gift horse—about to get a bullet between its eyes.

10:00 PM

It's been one day since Roxy was here, and it's started all over again—
the missing her, the mystery, the torment, my heart on fire. I want it
solved. I want it easy. I want to forget, or at least disregard everything
that's happened and whatever she's been doing since and just have
that night with all of us on the bed again.

Have you heard the story of Doctor Faustus, Sheriff? It's the
"deal with the devil" idea from a play, an Elizabethan tragedy from
the 1500s, written by Christopher Marlowe. Faustus is a scholarly
professor, philosopher, and scientist who becomes bored with his
own mastery of all intellectual skills and turns to the learning of
magic and witchcraft for stimulation. This entwines him with the
Good Angel and the Bad Angel, and he eventually makes a pact with
Lucifer to be given twenty-four years of magical powers in return
for his soul's damnation at the end of the term.

Faustus is ebullient and says, "All things that move between the
quiet poles shall be at my command!" Can you imagine having that
power? Through the years, the Good Angel tries to convince Faustus
to repent and cancel the deal with Lucifer. He considers it, as he's been
told that God is all forgiving, but he ultimately decides against it. The
satisfaction of the wizardry, the joy and power and succulent com-
pleteness with which he's so drunken are all too much to live without,
even if only temporarily, as long as he still has one more tomorrow.

There's a god-awful, cartoonish movie version of it from the
'60s out there directed by and starring Richard Burton. I love Burton, but that passion project got away from him. He even cast Liz
Taylor as Faustus's lover-ideal, Apollo. How many times were they
married, Burton and Taylor? At least twice, right? No wonder he
drank so much. And I drink so much, which I have to think about.
I'm not saying getting back with Roxy is a deal with the devil, Sheriff. Maybe it's a bad example. But what I'm talking about is doing
anything, giving anything, trading *anything*, conjuring *anything* for
love—to have it—the ideal—to destroy the not having of it like
Faustus desired—and Burton. Right now, I want more. And I too
want my Apollo. For real though. A real person, not thoughts or

fantasy to Internet bullshit. No more of that, especially after having touched Roxy again. And thanks for the offer, but I don't want to repent, even if my soul be damned.

11:45 PM

I don't know. Maybe it would be a deal with the devil. Or some kind of bad deal with myself. I mean, Faustus doesn't exactly have a happy ending. If Lucifer is known for one thing, it's keeping his damn promises.

I did get kicked in the teeth. That night at karaoke by myself, the thoughts that went through my head, ending it all. I could never tell anyone that. But I survived it. I guess. But maybe only on the thought of being back with her. Or, shit—maybe it was just because I knew I had to come back home to walk the damn dogs, I don't know. But I did love having Roxy here again. Holding someone and being held. Is it worth it? What is it worth? I'd thought it was everything. She thought it was less. Can less be everything again?

March 2, 9:30 AM

It happened quickly, with no warning, just like when she fell. There was a knock on the door this morning and her voice calling out, "Richard . . . Richard!" but this time also "I want to see my babies!"

The dogs went nuts. Lauren was beside herself. I shook the penny can. Didn't work. She knows her non–authority figure is back. I got them out of the Dignity Box and put it back in the bedroom so Irene wouldn't see it. I leashed them up and prepared to open the door.

Then I stopped, opened the door just a crack where I saw that Fay was standing with her. "I'll bring them over in a minute," I said. "Why don't you go over to your place, and I'll be there in a few."

"What have you done with my lovelies?" Irene squeaked. "You can't kidnap my children, Richard."

I chuckled politely. "How are you?" I asked through the screen where we'd first met.

"Oh, it's awful. They don't know what they're doing. My arm is killing me. I can't even move it, my neck either," she said.

How could I have expected anything other than misery?

"Well, at least you're home now," I said. All of the anxiety rebounded with the realization that life was boomeranging back to where it had been. People don't change. "You and Fay go ahead to your place, and we'll be right over."

I didn't want to be there for the big reveal, mostly because I didn't want it to be a big reveal. Maybe Fay, with the wisdom of her near nine decades, will keep it low key if Irene gets upset. Then I'll swoop in with the smiling dum-dums. Plus, I need a few minutes to brush them up and walk them, real quick. I want them to look like they were ready for a calendar shoot, and also not to pee on anyone's foot.

10:30 AM

The last walk. Irene had been gone for sixty-six days, over nine weeks, not enough time for Nelson to get trained, but enough time for me to not want to let them go. I'm finally walking them without having to clip the leashes to my belt loop. No more painter's mask and rubber gloves. They've even mapped out their favorites places to sniff and pee.

We ran the whole block around the elementary school, and then kept going south on Edinburgh. It was a long walk. I wanted to see if we could bump into Shadow, and Austen, or Elise, or Nathan, or Casino. I wanted to hear them say how good the dogs looked before they go back to no baths—even just a nod from Shadow would help.

We went down to Melrose Avenue. I love the contrast of their tiny bodies scurrying along against the buses that mope and the cars that zoom by on the busy street. Tourists always comment on how cute the dum-dums are. There's a billboard on the corner at Fairfax, an ad for NYB jeans. That rock chick always reminded me of Roxy's nighttime side. The perfect smile, the perfect presentation, but a little dirty too, and smart. We walked past the high school and stood in front of the West Melrose Apparel shop windows, the mannequins there, perfect and still, frozen in moments of comfort and pleasure. I used to window-shop for Roxy here because what looked good on them looked perfect on her in her perfect world. Well, I'm not perfect.

And I don't want to be perfect. I look down at the dogs who are tugging at their leashes because they're frightened by the traffic. And you know what? They're not perfect either. They're never going to be. Irene isn't perfect. Our living arrangement isn't perfect. This town isn't perfect, and neither are you, Sheriff. I don't want to live trying to fit into someone's fairy tale perfect world. That's not fair. Roxy only wanted me to get my shit together. And it isn't. Maybe I'm just not a shit-together-guy. Maybe I never will be. And she knows she's not perfect either. Who—ever, really, deep down—actually has their shit together? No one. I moved out here for a fairy tale. It doesn't exist. This is what my life is now, and I'm going to have to decide that I love it for what it is, and eventually I'll be loved for who I am—not who I was going to be, or who I am supposed to be—and love will change with me, not vice versa. Parmenides's philosophy was wrong.

Unfortunately, we didn't see Shadow today, but we did run into Elise and Austen. It felt good to hear them gush over the dogs.

"Oh, I can see that you're sad," Elise said.

"Of course, he is," said Austen. "You can't do what he did for these dogs and not feel like they're your family. You are a wonderful father, Richard."

He had no idea of the impact of that statement.

"They're happy that Irene is home," I said.

"They are, will be, missing you so, so, so much," Elise said, struggling with her English.

"Well, I'll miss them."

"You are such a good man," she said.

"Thanks."

"You can still go see them, right?" Austen asked.

"I actually hadn't thought about that. Irene and I aren't really friends, and now she's pissed about the haircuts."

"Well," Austen said, "you were just too good to her, and she'll just have to get over that and appreciate you. Plus, they look adorable."

"The Im-paws-able Dream, right?" I joked.

"Come true," he said.

Then, "You know something, Elise?" I said.

"Yes?"

"Did you know I used to be an English teacher?"

"No, oh—I didn't know that," she said.

"If you'd like, I can help you get over the hump with your English, your pronunciation."

"The—over what?"

"I can help you, if you like?"

"Oh . . . that would be wonderful. But I am so embarrassed sometimes."

"I can solve that."

"I didn't know. I can pay you," she said.

"Actually, that'd be a big help. We can help one another."

"And maybe, on the same days, you can teach my daughter to play guitar in the home? Austen told me you were a musician. She wants so much to play."

I gave her my number. That could be an extra $100 or more a week. That's health insurance. And then maybe find a couple more students. Why hadn't I thought of this?

We got back to the apartment. I was feeling strong. I thought about Doctor Faustus. Really, I thought about Richard Burton. Why did he want to do *Faustus*? What was he saying? It was that he, himself, was a tormented man. That's why he was drawn to it. He could cast his ephemeral Apollo, the real-life Elizabeth Taylor, in his movie, but he couldn't find a magical power in the real world to make her completely his if that's not what she wanted. There is no wizardry to summon but that which is our own willingness to see light and to change—and to wish well the change in others if it is to be.

I realized that my mind was made up. After I drop off the dogs, I would come back here and call Roxy, and tell her to please move on, that since she doesn't want me all the way, she needs to get out of my life for good, take me out of her contacts, no more texting, calls, or visits—nothing. She wanted it done. Let's be done.

Stasya would say, "Love is love." But sometimes it's not. I can't just be an option, living like cells under a microscope. I realize that my own stagnation has played a big part in this, but I feel I have to figure out the way forward on my own, be my own trusted partner. If Roxy and I can be friends eventually, that'll come as it comes. I know I can't do that right now. There are a few days left on my deposit on that ring. That was never going to happen, was it? Some other girl with a size 4½ and vintage sensibilities will love getting it one day.

Outside of Irene's door, I took a deep breath of fresh air, an old habit from my early days preparing to step inside there, and then I knocked. Fay let me in.

"Well, there he is—the man of the hour," Fay's wrinkled voice creaked out in chorus with the metal hinge of the door behind me.

Is that sarcasm? I wondered. *Can people that old still be sarcastic?*

As a kid, whenever I was in trouble and didn't know it yet, when I walked into a room where my father was, he'd always say, "There he is—himself," the opening gavel of a kangaroo court.

"And the doggies!" Fay continued with a half-alive smile.

Lauren started barking, but my penny can hand was empty. I glanced instinctively toward the kitchen to see if anyone had peed.

I unleashed the dum-dums, and they ran to Irene, who was sitting in her wing chair. She was as pale as the clean kitchen floor. Even in her energetic response to the dogs, she looked tired and worn like Elise's Omar. Her right arm hung limp like my father's after his stroke. She yanked each dog by the scruff with her left hand and set them on her lap. They danced like leprechauns and lapped their tongues against her cheeks as if she were a pork-flavored lollipop. Even their excitement couldn't bring any color to Irene's face. Before, I'd figured her to be about seventy-five; now she seemed older than sadness. She was trying to smile. The dogs forced her to. But I could see she was depressed, maybe beaten down on meds.

There was also a physical therapist there helping Irene get set up with exercise bands on the rear of her front door. I walked by her and hurried back to the bedroom. I opened the bureau top drawer, stuffed the gun into the back of my jeans and pulled my sweatshirt down. Tonight might be a rough night for Irene, and I didn't want that revolver within arm's reach. At that moment, I also didn't want a poorly maintained, half-loaded pistol in my pants, cold, and nuzzling its way into the crack of my ass. But if I didn't grab it now, I wouldn't get another chance. Maybe she won't remember that the gun was there in the first place. And from the flimsy look of her arm, she couldn't use it to protect herself even if she needed to. I'll talk to Randall again about getting bars on our windows.

I headed back out to the front room, realizing that I'd just shown a familiarity with Irene's apartment that she probably wasn't ready for. We hardly even knew each other, and here she'd returned to a clean place with all of her precious worthless crap suddenly vanished because of me.

With a chance to look, I realized that the physical therapist was adorable—Penelope Cruz in nursing scrubs and a spring jacket. She touched my forearm with her hand, tilted her head slightly to the right, looked at me, and said, "You did all this and took care of these two cuties while Irene was gone? You must be the sweetest man in the world."

Am I, Sheriff? Maybe I am.

"He cut my puppies' hair. He's a terrible person," Irene interjected, jokingly, from deep within her own sick truth.

"I love Yorkies with short hair," the physical therapist said. "I think they look like happy little puppies."

An ally. Very nice. "What's your name?" I asked.

"Natalia," she said. "I'll be helping Irene transition home. I'll be here on Tuesdays and Thursdays."

"I'll be here every day," I responded.

"He lives next door," Irene said. "Contrary to what you might think, we don't live together as a couple." Busting my balls was bringing color back to Irene's face.

Natalia went to Irene's chair and stroked the side of Nelson's face with the backs of her fingers. He turned and looked at me as if I owed him something for bringing Natalia here. *Let's just see how this goes, my friend.*

I excused myself, as my quick exit had gone on long enough. When I stepped outside, it was over. The dogs were gone, back to Irene, back to that life. All that was before me was the empty battlefield of the thin grass of the front yard, smothered in desert sunlight, fighting its way into rightful springtime—there where we began our training, and the parkway by the curb where Lauren got her first Treat for Pee, the whole sidewalk up and down North Hayworth. This was our tiny world, the treadmill that spun under our feet through so many walks for sixty-some sudden days. It got us all into shape. Will they remember any of it? Will they do the right thing without my encouragement on top of them?

"Richard, are you all right?" I heard Fay's slow voice whisper. I was still standing there in front of Irene's door. She came outside. "Richard, I just want to thank you for everything you've done. Irene, underneath it all, is a proud woman, and stubborn. She's lost so much in her life. It may take a little while for her to properly voice her appreciation, so I wanted to thank you for her."

"How's she really doing?"

"It's not good. She may need a surgery on her arm, which would send her back into the hospital for a while. The doctor doesn't want to put her through it. It'd involve a titanium rod that would go from her shoulder down to her elbow, so he's in a wait-and-see mode, hoping that her bones heal. It's not the bones though, really, it's her bad balance. The scales have finally tilted, and they don't see it getting any better. I hope Natalia's a help, but I don't know."

I had to refrain from any comments begrudging the brutality of aging in the presence of a woman more than ten years Irene's senior.

"Well, thanks for letting me know."

"Are you all right?" she insisted.

Apparently, I'm not hiding something. "Yes," I smiled.

"You're going to miss the dogs," she said. "Oh, that little Nelson, he's just—"

"Yeah . . . I suppose," I said. "I hope they stay clean. It's nutty how life turns out."

"Yes, it is. It is. Well, now you can have your life back."

"Yep."

She let me go then and returned inside. I came back to my place—my life—sat down on the sofa, and cried.

April

April 2, 8:00 PM

It was a painfully quiet afternoon. I'll never forget it. I go over and over it. All the silence I'd wished for was now mine, and I hated it. I decided not to call Roxy about a hundred times that day. One more day, and maybe . . .

But I did call her that evening and told her that I'd decided we should stay apart. She was unpleasantly surprised, which almost made me give in, but we talked it out, and I let her know that the hurt had been too much, I couldn't go back, and that I couldn't fully trust what going forward would be. And I know I was hurting her by not stepping up. From what I've learned, I finally told her, I have a lot of work to do on myself—figure myself out.

It's been over four weeks, and we haven't spoken since. It's been a giant dividing line. I couldn't even write in this log about it. Just silence and space—some sort of new life—but with one new element.

About two hours after that phone call with Roxy, I couldn't take being as alone as I felt. I walked over to Irene's door. The chandelier lights were on, and the storm door was slightly open behind the security screen. I could see her sitting in her wing chair, reading a book. I knocked. Then I knocked loudly. "Irene, it's Richard." I repeated it a few times until she responded.

"What?"

Maybe she'd been asleep. "It's me—Richard from next door."

"Oh . . ."

"I was wondering if I could come in and say hi to the dum-dums."

"Oh, OK, sure, come in."

I used my own key.

"I wish you wouldn't call them dum-dums," she said as I entered.

The dogs ran to me at the door, jumping, Lauren squealing as if she were trying to form vowels.

"These dogs are very smart, and they resent your insulting them."

"Any dogs that pee and poop inside are dum-dums." I stooped down to pet them. "So, until they change that, that's what they are in my book. Actually, I had them going outside pretty much 100 percent of the time after a while."

"They need a walk now, and I just can't do it. If you'd like to take them, feel free. Fay told me you were very good with the dogs, which at first shocked me because, and I told her this: 'No, he hates them! He'll be terrible!'"

"Well, the dogs did learn some dignity and self-respect."

Irene laughed. I hooked them up and took them for their night-time walk. We trotted along under the non-starry, big-city sky and the glowing streetlamps. It was business as usual. When I got back, Irene and I chatted about her recovery, how she was doing. She loved telling me stories about the Nazi and other patients at the home. I brought her my bag of dog treats and explained the vitals of Treats for Pee. She said she'd try. I told her all about Roxy. I was amazed at Irene's compassion and insight. Working through those divorces of her own, as well as her clients', really did give her wisdom. She said it's all for the best. Everything happens for a reason. When someone in her condition tells you that—rather than just the people doing well who spout that crap—it's a little easier to swallow.

I've gone over there every night since. She tells me, "Don't even knock anymore—what would you be interrupting?" I walk the dogs. You may see us some time if you're on night patrol. They give me guaranteed happiness once a day. Then I visit with Irene. I drop the dum-dums on the bed if she is up there reading or resting in the new armchair pillow that Casino replaced. Sometimes I grab the 409 and spend a minute in the kitchen wiping around. I can't stand the clean falling back.

I've shown her my chart. She thinks I have OCD. I still need her counsel in getting over Roxy, and the dogs still need my help getting over their bad habits and lazy desires. Irene is even shaking the penny can when Lauren barks, albeit with the force of a tranquilized butterfly. It's not as frequent as it was, because Irene never leaves anymore. They've taken her driver's license.

Natalia stops by my place after she's worked with Irene, but I'm taking it very slowly. I need to winter the troops before we march again. I want to be healed. (Ally sent me some Gua Lou Pi and Xiang Fu.) I will give Natalia this though, she's got me playing guitar again, singing my songs for her, and that feels good.

So, Sheriff, this six months of dog log worked. Life did change. Grand salute to the deputy who advised me on the phone back in October. I wish I'd gotten his name. If you can track that down, please offer him a promotion. Our problems are officially resolved and my complaint is hereby rescinded.

And it's a bit of a miracle, too. I have three new friends—Nelson, Lauren, and Irene—who love me and need me, whom I need and love, who have been there all the time. Forty feet away—just on the other side of the "good fence."

In fact, I have many new friends in the neighborhood, and, to think, the only time I went outside before was to go to my car to leave it.

So I'm not going to turn this in. I'm sure you're too busy to read happy endings. I should revisit my above statement, however: I've got four new friends, not three, because you—without ever knowing it or knowing me—have had an effect on my life, just by listening. That has changed me forever. I've worked some things out. I've gotten halfway to halfway.

So, I thank you, my friend. It has been an honor, sir, or ma'am. All the best.

Afterword

Some time has passed since the events described in this book. My friendship with Irene has become very special, very close, with night-time visits and dog walking, and meaningful, often very fun discussions about our lives past, present, and future. We share our hopes, and we share our gripes. She has helped me through good times and bad, many attempts and many failures. Unfortunately, she has fallen and/or needed some kind of surgery and convalescence several times over the years, and I continued taking Nelson and Lauren into my care each time.

The good news is, I was able to keep up their training. I got Lauren to stop barking at the front door, and both of them eventually stopped peeing inside—unless I stepped out and left them on their own, which I believe was more of a message to me than an accident. But I'll never know . . .

The bad news is that life is also difficult, as time inevitably steals our vitality. My best little buddy, Nelson, passed away in August 2016, and it's a hole in our hearts that Irene and I still acknowledge regularly. (He was, by the way, named after Irene's favorite professor at Vassar.) Nelson's ashes sit on Irene's bookshelf next to a framed photo of him in front of a martini at the Fat Dog, and if they ultimately pass to me, I will keep them with me always. Since Nelson's death, circumstances have become more and more challenging for Irene, so I've had Lauren in my care the majority of the time. Thankfully, Randall has been OK with me having the dogs in my apartment and has been more understanding toward Irene.

Lauren and I have had lots of fun with posts on social media as people have learned how our odd pairing came to be. She is sitting on my lap right now as I type this a few months before publication, just as she and Nelson both insisted on being on my lap, all three of us together on those chilly mornings when I was first typing away at turning this experience into a book. I hope there's a way that you can meet Lauren, because she's a real darling.

If you're interested in my old album *L.A. Never Dies*, which I kept saying was so great but never got a record deal—well, you can judge for yourself now, as we've rereleased it and it's available digitally everywhere. It remains untouched in its complete, original format, even the overambitious photo of the younger me on the cover. I hope there's lots there for you to enjoy.